EWS

From Privatisation to DB

Paul Shannon

Contents

First published 2012

ISBN 9780711035201

Published by Ian Allan Publishing
An imprint of Ian Allan Publishing Ltd, Hersham, Surrey KT12 4RG
Printed in England by Ian Allan Printing Ltd, Hersham, Surrey KT12 4RG

Visit the Ian Allan website at
www.ianallanpublishing.com

Distributed in the United States of America and Canada by BookMasters Distribution Services.

Acknowledgements
All photographs were taken by the author, unless otherwise accredited. I am grateful to Gavin Morrison and Hugh Ballantyne, who loaned photographs for use in this book, and to the many railway employees who helped by providing information and checking the manuscript. Any errors are the author's.

Bibliography

Baker, S. K. *Rail Atlas of Great Britain and Ireland*, various editions (Oxford Publishing Company)
Jacobs, Gerald (ed.) *British Rail Track Diagrams* (Quail Map Company)
Modern Railways (various issues)
Rail (various issues)
Rail Express (various issues)
Railways Illustrated (various issues)

FRONT COVER See page 57

BACK COVER TOP See page 59

BACK COVER BOTTOM See page 84

PREVIOUS PAGE 67028 leads the four-coach 13.17 London Marylebone to Wrexham train into Gobowen station on 14 May 2008. Sister locomotive 67013 is bringing up the rear.

Introduction

THE FORMATION OF ENGLISH Welsh and Scottish Railways Ltd marked a defining chapter in the history of British railfreight. It offered the hope of a fresh start after many years of decline under BR management, driven by stringent government targets which had forced a cautious, conservative approach. Thankfully, the government's intention to sell railfreight off in small chunks was not realised. If it had been, then in all probability the decline of railfreight would have continued as the different operators competed with each other instead of fixing their sights on the real competitor: road.

The first few years of EWS were almost too good to be true. Within weeks of its formation, the company announced £250 million worth of investment in 250 new locomotives, a move which showed that EWS's owners were in for the long haul, not just instant profits. The decision to reopen York wagon works and build 2,500 new wagons added to the confident, forward-looking message given out to existing and potential customers.

While part of EWS's policy was a continued drive for efficiency – the company planned to reduce its workforce from 7,600 to around 5,200 – it was the desire for growth that grabbed the headlines. The bold aim to double railfreight in five years and triple it in ten seemed achievable in view of the rapid growth EWS achieved in its first year, with 15% more

ABOVE 60083 has plenty of power to spare as it deputises for the rostered Class 37 on the 09.25 Warrington Arpley to Chirk timber train on 29 August 1997. The location is Rossett, on the single line between Saltney Junction and Wrexham. Although a short train such as this can scarcely have been profitable, the flow later developed into regular trainload business.

ABOVE Arriva Trains Wales made a number of Class 67-hauled driver-training runs on the North Wales Coast line in preparation for a proposed loco-hauled service between Holyhead and Manchester. 67014 is seen here passing Hargrave with one of the training runs from Holyhead to Crewe on 23 October 2007. Unfortunately, the planned service was cancelled on grounds of cost.

trains running in mid-1997 than when the company was formed in early 1996.

But where would the new business come from? Probably not from the traditional Trainload Freight markets such as coal and steel, given the shift away from coal-fired power stations and the likelihood of cutbacks at British Steel. In any case, BR had charged some of its key trainload customers high prices which were not sustainable on the privatised railway. Even the building materials market offered relatively few openings for new high-volume flows.

Instead, EWS would concentrate on developing new markets which rail had barely touched. Fast-moving consumer goods were a particular target – even if EWS gained only a small share of the 300 million tonnes of food and drink moved around the UK each year, it would make a tremendous difference to the railway's portfolio. Road congestion and environmental concerns would work in the favour of rail, as would the trend towards consolidating national and regional distribution centres.

The return of wagonload freight – under the marketing name 'Enterprise' which had been coined by Transrail – was for a time the jewel in EWS's crown. While the company was aware of the pitfalls of prolific trip workings and underused marshalling yards, Enterprise won a lot of new business, some of which would later form full trainloads. By mid-1997, Enterprise would be carrying almost 1.5 million tonnes of freight a year and new flows were appearing throughout the network.

The euphoria subsided after the departure of EWS Chairman Ed Burkhardt in 1999. Traffic had grown and cost savings had been achieved, but a question mark hung over the profitability of some train services, especially on the outer reaches of the Enterprise network. It was also a fact that EWS could no longer assume railfreight would automatically come its way. Freightliner was now taking a large slice of the infrastructure business and competing with increasing success for a range of bulk flows.

In the first years of the 21st century signals were mixed. On the one hand, EWS had fulfilled its investment plans with delivery of the last Class 66 and 67 locomotives and it was still winning some high-profile traffic flows. On the other hand, the company was dogged by problems such as concerns over quality of service, industrial relations issues and the Channel Tunnel/asylum seekers crisis. The Customer Service Delivery Centre at Doncaster did not live up to expectations, while the breakthrough into fast moving consumer goods was anything but fast, with a number of 'successful trials' failing to generate long-term business. The decision by Royal

Mail to cease using rail services was also a cruel blow.

The year 2005 saw a shrewd business move in the shape of Euro Cargo Rail, which built up an array of freight operations beyond the Channel – but not running through it – with astonishing speed. Another benefit was that it provided work for a large cohort of Class 66s that might otherwise have been standing idle in the UK. Some knowledgeable observers have suggested that Euro Cargo Rail saved EWS from bankruptcy as the firm's core business declined.

The final chapter in the EWS story was the takeover by DB Schenker, announced in June 2007 and taking effect later that year. The fact that Schenker was in no hurry to rebrand its new UK arm – the company was still officially EWS until January 2009 – was perhaps an indication of its motives. It was far more interested in gaining Euro Cargo Rail, with its strong competitive position in France, than in taking over the UK operation. Another sign of Schenker's cautiousness in the UK was in continuing the rundown of wagonload freight – quite an irony for a company which publicly championed wagonload on its home European territory. At the time of writing, the Chief Executive of DB Schenker's UK operation is based in Paris, along with the key directors of finance and public affairs – an indication of what really matters to DB.

ABOVE As part of the wagonload rundown, EWS reorganised its scrap metal traffic to run in block trains wherever possible. 66127 heads south at Filton with train 6C89, the 16.40 from Newport Alexandra Dock Junction to Tavistock Junction, on 4 June 2008. The MBA wagons would be tripped from Tavistock Junction to Plymouth Cattewater for reloading.

LEFT 66194 shunts empty hopper wagons at Wool before departing with 6Z15, the 18.55 to Neasden, on 17 July 2000. The derelict station goods yard at Wool was an unlikely starting point for a new railfreight flow, but was fortunately still usable when EWS won the contract to move sand from the nearby Warmwell quarry.

one

The Background

On 1 April 1994 the first step towards railfreight privatisation took place, as BR's freight operations were restructured in preparation for the eventual sell-off. Trainload Freight – which had been established in 1987 with four sub-sectors, Coal, Construction, Metals and Petroleum – was divided into three new divisions: TLF North East, TLF South East and TLF West. These would be vested as separate BR subsidiary companies in April 1995.

Initially the boundaries between the divisions were geographical, as their names suggest, but the long-term intention was to promote competition across the network, with each company free to bid for all available business whether pre-existing or new. The geographical allocation was based on the starting point of each traffic flow, except in the case of coal where destination was the deciding factor.

The three new Trainload Freight divisions also acquired the Contract Services business of Railfreight Distribution (RfD). This included various trainload flows of chemicals, industrial minerals, timber, paper and edible products, as well as BR's departmental services which supplied the railway infrastructure with materials such as ballast, sleepers and rail.

Unaffected by the Trainload Freight restructuring were the remaining divisions of Railfreight Distribution, comprising Freightliner, European, automotive and Ministry of Defence traffic. Freightliner would be offered for sale as a separate business, while automotive traffic was expected to integrate naturally with RfD's European business once the Channel Tunnel was open. Ministry of Defence traffic was expected to become mainly intermodal in nature. Rail Express Systems – formed in 1991 to take charge of mail, parcels and charter work – remained a separate entity.

The starting point in forming TLF North East, TLF South East and TLF West was to create three divisions roughly equal in terms of size. However, the North East and South East divisions generated a larger profit than TLF West because they handled a larger share of core trainload business, especially delivering coal to power stations.

As far as possible, the three divisions would be managed and administered on similar lines. Each division was tasked to produce its own safety case, which would need to be approved by Railtrack before its licence was awarded. Railtrack itself had taken control of the railway infrastructure, on 1 April 1994, and would be floated on the Stock Exchange in May 1996.

TLF North East

Headed by Ian Braybrook, who had latterly worked as a Trainload Freight director in charge of restructuring, TLF North East occupied a smaller area than the other two divisions – taking in North East England, Yorkshire and Humberside. The reason for the small size was the inclusion of several very large traffic centres, notably the port of Immingham and the steel plants at Scunthorpe and Teesside. However, many of the division's trains would travel to destinations outside the home area, requiring close cooperation with the other freight divisions.

TLF North East's resources included 33 Class 60 locomotives – the 100-strong fleet was shared as equitably as possible between the three divisions – and a varied selection of Classes 56, 47 and 37. Traction maintenance depots were located at Blyth, Thornaby, Knottingley, Healey Mills, Doncaster and Immingham, with wagon repair depots operating at the same locations bar Blyth and Healey Mills, plus the addition of Tyne Yard. Operationally, TLF North East was divided into two regions, North East and Yorkshire/Humberside, each having its own manager and administrative staff.

Coal accounted for just over half of TLF North East's income, with the three Aire Valley power stations at Drax, Eggborough and

LEFT Transrail used its electric train heating-fitted Class 37 locomotives to provide haulage for selected passenger trains on the North Wales Coast. 37407 *Blackpool Tower* passes Penmaenmawr with the 12.24 from Crewe to Holyhead on 24 June 1995.

RIGHT Rail Express Systems operated charter trains alongside its mail operations. 47758 heads west between Chester and Saltney Junction on 30 April 1994, with the Nenta Traintours 'North Wales Coastliner' excursion from Norwich to Llandudno.

LEFT 60056 *William Beveridge* passes Hunslet yard, Leeds – carrying Trainload Freight livery but devoid of subsector decals – with train 6M54, the 10.56 from Leeds to Stanlow, on 18 February 1995. Transrail operated bulk oil trains from Stanlow to several destinations, but this was a declining market as Shell gradually pulled out of rail transport in favour of pipelines and road-tanker deliveries.

Ferrybridge as the major destinations. Drax alone took up to 30 coal trains a day, sourced both from the massive Selby coalfield loading point at Gascoigne Wood and from smaller pits such as Prince of Wales, Kellingley, Maltby and Harworth. Imported coal was only just beginning to make an impact. Other coal delivery destinations served by TLF North East included Cambois power station, Scunthorpe steelworks, Hope cement works and the ICI chemicals plant at Wilton. The medium-term prospects for coal traffic in the TLF North East area were relatively strong, although an early challenge came in the form of open access operations by National Power, depriving the division of some of its most lucrative business between Gascoigne Wood and Drax.

TLF North East's steel traffic included the intensive shuttle of iron ore trains from Immingham to Scunthorpe and a range of semi-finished products from Scunthorpe to Lackenby, Rotherham and Wolverhampton. The British Steel Teesside complex took trainloads of limestone and lime from Hardendale and produced a large number of outgoing flows, including slabs to Dalzell, Workington and Shelton and coil to Corby, Wakefield, Blackburn and Wolverhampton. Smaller but significant centres for steel traffic included the United Engineering Steels complex at Aldwarke and the Avesta plant at Tinsley.

Lindsey and Humber refineries at Immingham produced a steady stream of block oil trains, serving destinations mainly in the Midlands and northern England, as well as taking deliveries of crude oil from the Lincolnshire oilfield. The Phillips refinery at Port Clarence provided additional trainloads of petroleum. Chemicals traffic included acetic acid from Saltend and styrene monomer from Immingham. Further freight flows out of Immingham included imported paper to Barking and fertiliser to several regional distribution depots.

The construction industry formed a small part of TLF North East's portfolio, with just one major quarry at Rylstone falling within its catchment area. However, the division also operated the then recently acquired flow of containerised desulphogypsum from Drax to Kirkby Thore. Former RfD Contract Services flows operated by TLF North East included blocks from Heck and salt and potash from Boulby.

In readiness for its vesting as a separate company, TLF North East was the first of the three divisions to gain a new identity, launched at the Doncaster Works open day on 9 June 1994. The name Loadhaul was chosen for its conciseness and geographical anonymity. A striking orange and black livery produced by

RIGHT Loadhaul had the most striking colour scheme of the three pre-privatisation divisions of Trainload Freight. Freshly repainted locomotive 56003 passes Burton Salmon with empty merry-go-round wagons, on its way from Drax to Milford West sidings on 18 February 1995.

ABOVE 47332 heads south at Winwick with 6F47, the 12.37 Enterprise train from Workington to Warrington Arpley on 3 May 1995. The load comprises two empty caustic soda tanks from Sellafield to Ellesmere Port, one empty nitric acid tank from Sellafield to Ince & Elton, and a consignment of steel rail from Workington to Tees Dock. Transrail's Enterprise trains produced varied combinations of wagon types that recalled the BR Speedlink network.

Venture Design was favoured, partly for practical reasons – these colours showed dirt less readily than others – and partly because neither colour had been routinely used in British locomotive liveries for a long time. Indeed, Loadhaul deliberately avoided using the traditional railway colours of green, blue, yellow and red. With bold blocks of colour running across the contours of the locomotive, it conveyed the message 'big and heavy'.

The first locomotives to carry full Loadhaul livery were Nos 37713 and 56039, while No 60050 had the Loadhaul logo applied to its existing Trainload Freight two-tone grey. Full repaints in orange and black were largely restricted to those locomotives with existing paintwork in poor condition, although by late 1995 five Class 37s, 23 Class 56s and three Class 60s had been treated.

TLF South East

Headed by Kim Jordan, previously Trainload Freight Director Coal, the South East area split naturally into two regions: the East Midlands and East Anglia, where coal was the dominant business; and the South and South East, with its emphasis on aggregates traffic. While the prospects for coal were not good, TLF South East anticipated significant growth in the aggregates business, as the construction industry recovered from the recession of the early 1990s and the South East had to look further afield for its supplies.

TLF South East's main locomotive depots were Toton, Stewarts Lane and Stratford,

LEFT 47391 and 47386 pass Ashford with empty vans returning from Neasden to France via the Channel Tunnel on 24 July 1995. Many RfD trains were rostered for double-headed Class 47s in order to enhance their reliability. The bottled water traffic to Neasden was a growth area at this time and often ran in whole trainloads.

ABOVE 56047 passes Ellesmere Port with 6P75, the 15.00 Lostock to Stanlow empty tank train, on 4 August 1995. The adjacent stabling point and sorting sidings were still busy at this time, but traffic would soon take a nosedive as Shell and nearby chemical companies abandoned rail. The Transrail logo was applied over various BR liveries, including the grey and yellow 'Civilink' scheme.

supported by inspection points at Leicester, Peterborough, Didcot, Hither Green and Eastleigh. Alongside its complement of 33 Class '60' locomotives, TLF South East took on the entire fleet of Class 58s, as well as a share of the Class 31, 37 and 47 fleets. The division also continued to operate Class 33 diesels and Class 73 electro-diesels on their traditional Southern Region territory, with the electro-diesels finding regular work on weekend engineering trains and on the flask train to Lydd.

In the Midlands, the Trent Valley power stations at West Burton, Cottam, Ratcliffe, Willington, Drakelow and Rugeley provided work for many of the Class 58s and 60s based at Toton. At that time much of the coal consumed in the Trent Valley came from the Nottinghamshire coalfield, while some came from locations in Yorkshire and Staffordshire. Other destinations for coal in the Midlands included Rufford stocking site and the Coalite plant at Bolsover. In its South and South East region, TLF South East supplied Didcot power station with imported coal from Avonmouth and delivered industrial coal to Ridham paper mill in North Kent.

The list of aggregates flows hauled by TLF South East was headed by the high-volume traffic from Merehead and Whatley quarries in the Mendips to various receiving depots in the South and South East. Using Class 59 locomotives owned by the quarry firms Foster

LEFT Railfreight Distribution managed to revive Vauxhall car traffic from Luton for a time, using the former Luton Crescent Road freight depot as the loading point. 47237 shunts car carriers at Crescent Road on 25 July 1994, before departing with train 4S48, the 17.45 to Bathgate.

Yeoman and ARC, TLF South East ran 3,000-tonne 'jumbo' trains from Merehead and Whatley to Acton yard, where they were split into portions for individual terminals. TLF South East also ran some direct trains from Merehead and Whatley to destinations such as Eastleigh, Theale and Wootton Bassett. Within the South East, aggregates flows operated from Angerstein Wharf, Cliffe and Marks Tey to various receiving terminals.

Further aggregates traffic was generated by the Leicestershire quarries at Mountsorrel, Croft, Bardon Hill and Stud Farm, with destinations ranging from Norwich and Banbury to Radlett and Angerstein Wharf. The haulage of these trains was shared by Classes 58 and 60, which meant that the '58s' now covered a much wider area than they had done in Trainload Coal days.

Cement traffic in the TLF South East area comprised a single flow from Ketton to King's Cross. Industrial sand was conveyed from Middleton Towers to glassworks at Worksop, Barnby Dun and Monk Bretton. Household waste generated four rail-borne flows in the South East: Cricklewood to Stewartby, Northolt to Calvert, Brentford to Appleford, and from three transfer stations in the Bristol/Bath area to Calvert.

Petroleum traffic from the North Thamesside refineries had already declined sharply before TLF South East came into being, leaving the division with residual traffic to locations such as Kilnhurst and Didcot. Further petroleum flows included North Sea oil condensate from North Walsham to Harwich, solvent from Harwich to Longport, liquid petroleum gas from Furzebrook to Avonmouth, crude oil from Holybourne to Fawley, liquid petroleum gas from Fawley to Longport and bitumen from Fawley to Bromford Bridge and Plymouth.

Metals traffic in the TLF South East area was limited to a small amount of traffic for CoSteel at Sheerness, including scrap from Snailwell and Willesden and occasional outward loads of finished steel.

In July 1994, TLF South East gained its new identity as Mainline Freight, following development work carried out by London-based corporate design specialists Halpin Grey Vermeir. In retrospect the name seems uncontroversial, but at the time it was carefully chosen to avoid any reference to railway geography – due to the division's nationwide aspirations – and words which referred only to one type of operation, such as 'trainload'. 'Mainline', on the other hand, immediately brought railways to mind and underlined the point that freight traffic was on the move, rather than skulking around in sidings.

ABOVE 60088 *Buachaille Etive Mor* passes Burton-on-Trent with a merry-go-round train from Nadins disposal point to Ratcliffe, on 10 August 1995. Mainline Freight rubbed shoulders with Transrail and Loadhaul on the busy cross-country route between Derby and Birmingham.

In contrast to the Loadhaul approach, Mainline Freight wanted to maintain railway design traditions and avoid any outlandish new livery. Blue and yellow were duly adopted, while the Mainline Freight logo comprised a sequence of superimposed wheels placed on a horizontal line – clearly and simply symbolising the idea of movement by rail.

While a trial version of the Mainline Freight logo was unveiled in July 1994, it was several more months before the full livery was revealed on No 58050 at the October 1994 London Freightconnection event. In due course it appeared on the core locomotive fleet, mainly Class 37s but also including some members of Classes 58, 73, 08, 09 and 60. The '33s' were excluded because of limited life expectancy.

TLF West

Under the leadership of Julian Worth, previously Trainload Freight Director Metals and Petroleum, TLF West covered a huge geographical area including the whole of Scotland, North West England, Wales, the West Midlands and South West England. The size of the area was both its strength and its weakness. While it gave the division a broad range of business which was less vulnerable to sudden change in a particular industry, it also meant that resources had to be provided over a large area with less chance of the economies of scale enjoyed by TLF North East at Immingham and TLF South East in the Mendips. TLF West also had a significantly greater headcount than the other two divisions.

For day-to-day operations, TLF West was divided into three regions: Scotland; North West and West Midlands; and South Wales and South West. Its commercial functions were arranged differently, with metals and coal contracts throughout the region managed from Cardiff and most other contracts managed from Manchester. The division's main traction maintenance depots were Motherwell, Wigan Springs Branch, Bescot, Cardiff Canton and St Blazey, with major inspection points at Millerhill, Ayr, Buxton and Margam. The depots

ABOVE 90134 passes Docker with 4M72, the 10.25 Mossend to Wembley intermodal train, on 29 October 1995 – one of three daily intermodal departures from Mossend at this time. Channel Tunnel traffic took off more slowly than BR had hoped, but in retrospect the early years were the busiest – before problems with asylum seekers exacerbated the already high costs and inconsistent performance of the service.

at Crewe and Saltley were placed under the management of Railfreight Distribution.

TLF West had more locomotives on its books than the other two divisions, including a significantly larger number of shunters and lower-powered Class 31s which were well suited to departmental (i.e. railway infrastructure) traffic. This was because the division covered a larger route mileage and therefore operated a larger number of departmental trains than the others. TLF West was also the only division to maintain fleets of Class 31/4 and 37/4 locomotives for hire to passenger train operating companies in the North West and Scotland.

TLF West's biggest concentration of coal traffic was in South Wales where, despite the

TLF North East: employees and rolling stock, 1994

Employees total	2,303
Locomotives:	
Class 60	33
Class 56	57
Class 47	24
Class 37	66
Classes 08/09	48
Total	**228**
Wagons:	
Coal	2,176
Metals	1,250
Infrastructure	1,662
Other	84
Total	**5,172**

TLF South East: employees and rolling stock, 1994

Train crew	1,118
Other employees	1,835
Main line locomotives:	
Class 60	33
Class 58	50
Class 47	15
Class 37	69
Class 33	21
Class 31	32
Class 73	25
Total	**245**
Wagons total	**7,344**

TLF West: employees and rolling stock, 1994

Train crew	1,580
Other employees	2,250
Locomotives:	
Class 60	34
Class 56	55
Class 47/0	22
Class 37/7	19
Class 37/5	21
Class 37/4	27
Class 37/0-3	54
Class 31	93
Classes 08/09	84
Total	**409**
Wagons:	
Coal	2,302
Metals	1,319
Contract Services	700
Infrastructure	5,000
Other	37
Total	**9,358**

mass closure of pits, the railway still supplied Aberthaw power station with coal from several opencast sites, as well as imported coal from Avonmouth. Further north, TLF West ran merry-go-round coal trains to Ironbridge and Fiddlers Ferry power stations, while in Scotland it served power stations at Cockenzie, Longannet and Methil.

Steel traffic in the TLF West area was dominated by British Steel's South Wales plants at Port Talbot, Llanwern, Trostre and Ebbw Vale. The division ran heavy block trains of raw materials and semi-finished steel between those plants, as well as longer-distance trains carrying lime from Hardendale and steel to Round Oak and Shotton. A more complex suite of services served the Allied Steel & Wire plant at Cardiff, carrying inward scrap and outward finished products for the construction industry.

TLF West carried large volumes of limestone from the Peak District quarries operated by RMC and Buxton Lime Industries, including the Brunner Mond Northwich flow which had previously belonged to RfD Contract Services. Cement traffic consisted of various flows for Blue Circle from Hope and Oxwellmains. Household refuse trains operated in the Manchester and Edinburgh areas.

The petroleum traffic handled by TLF West included trains from Stanlow, Grangemouth, Robeston, Waterston, Llandarcy and Cardiff. However, rail-borne petroleum traffic was in decline, especially from Stanlow.

Sellafield nuclear reprocessing plant was located in the TLF West area, where the division therefore took on the network of flask trains from nuclear power stations around the UK coast, still using the Class 31s Trainload Coal had introduced, as well as block trains of chemicals from Cheshire. The Sellafield traffic would gradually transfer to Direct Rail Services haulage from 1996 onwards.

TLF West became Transrail, the new name selected to reflect both the key role of **Trans**port by **Rail** and a strategy to seek business across the railway industry, not only freight. Given the likely short life of the three TLF companies, Transrail opted to retain the two-tone grey livery and applied its 'big T' logo on the base.

RIGHT 92012 *Thomas Hardy* passes Kensington Olympia with 6M34, the 13.45 Connectrail train from Dollands Moor to Wembley, on 24 July 1996. It took a long time to clear RfD's Class 92s to work the key electrified routes between the Channel Tunnel, London and northern England.

LEFT Loadhaul locomotive 56039 *ABP Port of Hull* heads south at Burton-on-Trent with train 6M99 from Scunthorpe to Wolverhampton Steel Terminal on 10 August 1995, carrying billet for distribution in the West Midlands.

two

Enter Wisconsin – A New Dawn for Railfreight

The first sign of what would become UK railfreight's 21st-century revolution came in late 1995, when American railroad Wisconsin Central emerged as the front runner to acquire Rail Express Systems, the BR sector in charge of Royal Mail and charter trains. RES was an attractive proposition, as it not only held a national licence for parcels traffic but was also the only company licensed to run passenger trains throughout the Railtrack network.

The sale of Rail Express Systems to a consortium led by Wisconsin Central was confirmed at 05.00 hours on 9 December 1995. The consortium was known as North & South Railways Limited and its chairman was Edward A. Burkhardt, an experienced US railroader who would soon set the pace of change in the UK railfreight industry. RES was the first BR operating company to be sold; at the time of its sale it employed 800 staff and owned a sizeable fleet of locomotives and rolling stock, as detailed in the table below. It also operated the Royal Mail's Class 325 electric units and the Royal Train coaches owned by Railtrack. However, the financial position of RES was far from secure, as it had recorded a £10 million loss on a turnover of £57.3 million in 1994/95, despite some major restructuring.

While day-to-day mail and charter operations continued as before, the new Wisconsin-led management was candid about the need to achieve and maintain profitability, primarily through cost savings. On a more positive note, investment in new diesel locomotives was also seen as a high priority.

The ink was barely dry on the RES contract when Wisconsin Central confirmed it was bidding for Loadhaul, Mainline Freight and Transrail. While the UK government had hoped to sell the three trainload freight companies as separate businesses to encourage competition – and all three management teams had formed their own management buyout companies – Wisconsin Central made it clear that it was interested only in acquiring the companies as a single entity which it would then integrate with Rail Express Systems. The only other bidder for the trainload businesses by December 1995 was FirstFreight, a consortium led by the management of Loadhaul and backed by Denver-based rail haulier OmniTRAX. But FirstFreight was soon relegated to second place and it was only a matter of time before the American-led takeover became reality.

In the early hours of 24 February 1996, contracts were signed to mark the sale of Loadhaul, Mainline Freight and Transrail to the Wisconsin Central consortium. The formal handover from British Railways Board Chairman John Welsby to Ed Burkhardt took place at a ceremony at London Marylebone station later the same day.

Rail Express Systems traction and rolling stock fleet, December 1995

Class 08	27
Class 47	117 (including 8 stored)
Class 86	15
Class 90	5
Class 307 driving cars*	58
Barrier wagons	8
Vans	611

*for conversion to propelling control vehicles

LEFT Trainload Coal-liveried locomotive 31201 passes Caledonian Road with the Thursdays-only Willesden to Southminster flask train on 13 June 1996. Nuclear flask traffic passed briefly through EWS hands before Direct Rail Services took over.

BELOW Foster Yeoman and ARC continued to use EWS crews to drive their Class 59 locomotives, working out of the Mendip quarries. 59104 *Village of Great Elm* approaches Willesden South West Sidings with the 12.09 Acton to Purfleet feeder service on 22 July 1996.

ABOVE Several cement works started to receive coal by rail in the 1990s, including the Castle works at Penyffordd where the rail connection had been out of use for several years. 08817 shunts one of the first trainloads of coal at Penyffordd on 20 July 1996, on this occasion coming from Hull.

The sale price was reported to be £225 million, a figure which some observers criticised as being too low as it represented only 10% of the companies' replacement value. On the other hand, no one was expecting UK railfreight to generate easy profits. Even before the sale was confirmed, Burkhardt talked of the need for significant cost savings (which inevitably meant job losses) in order for the industry to survive and flourish. On its home territory Wisconsin resourced as many tonne-miles as the three UK companies, but with only 1,700 staff rather than the total of nearly 7,000 employed by Loadhaul, Mainline Freight and Transrail.

When Ed Burkhardt presented his strategy to the UK press, his most attention-grabbing remark related to his commitment to wagonload freight. In contrast with the 'trainload' ethos BR had promoted, Burkhardt saw single wagon consignments as offering the best potential for growth. The core trainload flows would be nurtured as well, but most of the bulk freight markets were mature and the profit margins on some flows, notably coal, would inevitably be squeezed as nationalised industries gave way to private enterprise and real competition.

Burkhardt's first thoughts on how to tackle wagonload touched on the 'freight village' concept and the need to serve industrial customers' premises directly. Railtrack was seen as a hurdle, both in terms of the level of track access charges and of providing access to yards and sidings. The obvious way forward agreed by Burkhardt and his team was to build on Transrail's Enterprise network, which had grown significantly since its 1994 launch and now reached deep into Loadhaul and Mainline Freight territories. Burkhardt also indicated that a growing wagonload network was likely to require a revival of marshalling yards, although he stopped short of foreseeing a comeback of 1960s-style hump shunting.

Little was said about the prospects for intermodal traffic. The Wisconsin consortium had decided not to bid for Freightliner because it did not believe it could sustain profitability. On the other hand, Mainline Freight had crept into Freightliner territory by launching its own intermodal service from Harwich, while Transrail had launched Roadrailer services between Aberdeen and Northampton. In the privatised landscape, there was nothing to stop the new company from developing its own intermodal product.

As for traction, Ed Burkhardt had some practical yet quite radical ideas. Bottom of the pile

were the Class 47s, once the most numerous and flexible locomotive type in use with BR, but which were riddled with problems and best dispensed with as soon as replacements became available. The remaining Class 20s and Class 33s also faced early withdrawal, as did those non-refurbished Class 37s which remained in service. The Class 60s would retain their position as prime heavy haulers, while at the other end of the spectrum Burkhardt praised the humble Class 08 shunters as 'some of the most dependable machines in all creation!' Stored examples would be reinstated as and when necessary.

The company's intention to replace the lower-powered and life-expired members of its main-line locomotive fleet was confirmed by Burkhardt at the Edinburgh Railfreight Conference in April 1996. There would be two sub-classes of a new Class 61 (later amended to '66') design, one having a maximum speed of 75mph with slow speed control equipment for heavy freight work and the other with a maximum speed of 100mph for RES and passenger work. The fleet would number several hundred locomotives and was expected to be built in North America by General Motors,

ABOVE The glistening maroon and gold livery of visiting locomotive 56089 makes a fine sight, as it stands on the Severn Valley Railway turntable at Kidderminster on 13 October 1996. HUGH BALLANTYNE

BELOW Newly repainted 08921 stands inside Crewe works on 16 August 1996. The humble Class 08 shunter received a big vote of confidence from EWS management; the company even considered reinstating withdrawn examples if warranted by an increase in traffic. HUGH BALLANTYNE

ABOVE 37264 sets back into Forders Sidings, Stewartby, with wagonloads of spoil from weekend engineering work, on 21 March 1997. The recombination of Loadhaul, Transrail and Mainline Freight gave EWS the monopoly of Railtrack infrastructure traffic.

embracing the latest technology such as computer controls and electronic fuel injection.

With Wisconsin Central holding only a 33.3% share of the new company, the Wisconsin name would not feature in its corporate identity. The company initially traded as North & South Railways but soon opted for the title English Welsh & Scottish Railway Limited (EWS), neatly emphasising the nationwide scope of the company while not ruling out any particular kind of operation – freight or passenger.

To choose its logo, EWS ran two competitions – one for its own staff and one for readers of *Rail* magazine. The logo had not only to suit the new EWS colour scheme, which was maroon, but also to sit comfortably on older livery styles such as

ABOVE The Royal Mail contract dominated the Rail Express Systems business that Wisconsin Central took over in December 1995. A Class 325 unit crosses the River Weaver at Dutton on a down mail working on 8 July 1997.

Trainload's two-tone grey (as well as those of Mainline Freight and Loadhaul) which would be around for some time to come. The idea of a logo competition for 'amateurs' ruffled the feathers of the professional design firm Roundel, who had previously produced the award-winning but controversial red branding for RES.

While the competition was underway, EWS unveiled its locomotive livery at a press launch at Toton depot on 25 April 1996. The first recipient was No 37057, which had just undergone an 'F' exam. The dominant colour was maroon, as expected, but a darker shade than that used by Wisconsin in America or New Zealand. It was also relieved by a deep gold bodyside band, with a yellow reflective stripe running along the bottom of the bodyside. The acronym 'EW&S' (the '&' was later dropped) and locomotive number were positioned on the gold bodyside band, with space left under the driver's window for the yet-to-be-confirmed logo.

LEFT EWS managed to keep several rail-borne flows of household coal, including occasional trains to the Smallshaws yard at Gobowen. 37380 arrives at Gobowen with the 14.45 departure from Warrington Arpley on 4 June 1997, conveying coal in HEA hoppers.

By the end of May, EWS colours had been applied to members of Classes 56, 58 and 60, enabling some fine tuning to take place before the livery was rolled out on all locomotives receiving a heavy repair at works or a major depot. The company's new logo was revealed in September 1996: designed by professional illustrator Tom Connell, it was a stylised graphic incorporating the English lion, Welsh dragon and Scottish stag. It would form an integral part of the EWS identity, with full-colour or monochrome versions appearing on locomotives, wagons, depot signs, publicity material and stationery.

Meanwhile, the EWS locomotive renewal programme got underway. The company ordered 250 diesels from General Motors, including 30 high-geared examples with electric train heating, for delivery from late 1997 onwards. Roughly half of the fleet was earmarked for new business, with the remainder facilitating the withdrawal of older traction. The Export Development Corporation of Canada provided the initial funding for the locomotives to be built in Ontario, pending a £375-million leasing deal with Angel Train Contracts which would be agreed once they were in production.

The new locomotives shared the body profile of the GM Class 59s, but were mechanically based on the successful 4,000hp SD70MAC design which went into production in 1994. The decision to purchase foreign-built locomotives inevitably provoked opposition, but for EWS there was no realistic alternative – given that each new

EWS operational main-line locomotive fleet, March 1996

Class	Number
Class 31	70
Class 33	17
Class 37	237
Class 47	111
Class 56	116
Class 58	50
Class 60	100
Class 73	23
Class 86	15
Class 90	5
Total	**744**

GM locomotive would cost about half as much as the Brush Class 60, and would be cheaper and easier to maintain.

On 24 December 1996, EWS was named as the preferred bidder for Railfreight Distribution, having fended off an alternative bid from a consortium including Freightliner, Transfesa and Stagecoach. The main incentive for the bid was access to the Channel Tunnel, but the deal also included domestic automotive and Ministry of Defence traffic. The RfD takeover would provide a challenge for EWS, as RfD had generated an income of only £67 million in 1995/96 against costs of £123 million. The division also had many elderly assets on its books, including 72 Class 47s, which EWS was keen to replace as soon as possible.

The actual takeover of RfD did not take place until 22 November 1997, having been delayed by the need for approval by the European Community competition directorate. EWS also acquired all railway assets of the open-access operator National Power in April 1998, including six Class 59 locomotives, 106 bogie hopper wagons and Ferrybridge wagon repair depot. Although the freight tonnages involved were small, it was a reassuring vote of confidence by National Power in the nation's biggest railfreight operator.

EWS operational main line locomotive fleet, April 1998 (after acquiring RfD)

Class 31	27
Class 33	7
Class 37	203
Class 47	142
Class 56	109
Class 58	50
Class 59	6
Class 60	100
Class 73	22
Class 86	16
Class 87	1
Class 90	25
Class 92	46
Total	**754**

ABOVE Typical of many small freight flows that EWS developed in its early years was timber from Scotland to Pontrilas. A small amount of investment in re-fettling an existing refuge siding provided a convenient offloading point, with trains hauled by a RES Class 47 locomotive in marginal time. 47741 arrives at Pontrilas with 6C38, the 11.08 departure from Newport Alexandra Dock Junction, on 17 July 1997.

TOP RIGHT 58033, pictured at Toton depot on 28 July 1997, was the first member of its class to carry EWS livery. The gold bodyside band was higher than on later repaints and the acronym 'EW&S' had not yet given way to 'EWS'.
GAVIN MORRISON

BOTTOM RIGHT 59206, still working on its National Power homeground, crawls forward at Gascoigne Wood loading point with a train for Drax on 7 August 1998. The acquisition of National Power's railway assets was a significant vote of confidence for EWS, who wasted no time in repainting the six former Class 59/2 locomotives.

English Welsh & Scottish Railway
Toton
12
13
14
EW&S 58033
58033

EWS
59206

three

Strategy and Resources

With its acquisition of RfD concluded and little apparent competition from other railfreight companies, EWS was looking forward to a rosy future. Managing Director Ian Braybrook was proud of his company's achievements in its first 12 months. Specifically, EWS had committed almost £500 million to new resources including locomotives, wagons, a customer service centre and a replacement for the BR TOPS computer system. It had negotiated a new track access agreement with Railtrack, which offered price stability for the latter and a pricing regime which was simple, predictable and conducive to growth for the railfreight business. No less importantly, EWS had also agreed new conditions of employment with key groups of staff, offering higher basic salaries, better pensions and more varied jobs.

LEFT The Class 60s were EWS's flagship locomotives in the early days, some quickly repainted in EWS livery. 60051 passes Elford with 6E59, the 17.12 Kingsbury to Lindsey petroleum 'empties', on 19 August 1997. At this time Kingsbury handled up to two petroleum trains a day, both from the Immingham refineries.

EWS's structure built on the best practices of previous freight companies. Production functions were divided between three geographical regions, while commercial functions were geared toward commodities. Four of the commercial divisions mirrored those of Trainload Freight days, with general managers respectively responsible for minerals, metals, construction or petroleum and chemicals. The other three divisions reflected the extended business base of EWS: Business Development was led by Julian Worth, whose experience in developing the Enterprise network as Transrail MD placed him in a strong position to win new business, especially in the distribution and consumer goods sectors; Infrastructure Services took care of what had been non-commercial departmental traffic in BR days, but was now handled on the same commercial basis as other freight flows; Rail Express Services took charge of the Royal Mail contract and of non-freight operations such as charter work and stock moves.

EWS's capital investment programme started to bear fruit in early 1998 as its first new locomotive, No 66001, rolled off the General Motors production line, formally passing into EWS ownership on 23 March. It went into service at Immingham on 18 April and was briefly displayed to the press, before being moved to Toton and Derby for various tests and measurements to ensure compliance with specifications. It hauled its first load on the main line on 27 May and worked its first revenue-earning train on 2 June, from Toton to Drakelow power station and back.

The first delivery of production Class 66s took place at Newport Docks on 26 August, when Nos 66003/04/05 were offloaded from heavy lift vessel MV *Stellamare*. Type approval for the Class 66s had been gained 12 days previously, so the new arrivals could operate over the Railtrack network with minimal delay. Further Class 66 deliveries continued apace, with batches of up to 11 locomotives reaching Newport at roughly three-weekly intervals. However, the proposal to build a high-speed variant of the '66' was dropped because of concerns about excessive track forces, with the order changed to 250 heavy-haul locomotives.

To facilitate mail trains and other high-speed services, EWS placed a fresh order with GM for 30 Class 67 locomotives to be built by Alstom in Spain under licence. They would have a maximum speed of 125mph, instead of 100mph as originally planned. Unlike the Class 66s, which shared many features (including their body outline) with the existing Class 59s, the '67s' were built to an entirely new design with a weight-saving monocoque structure and would therefore need to undergo full Railtrack safety case approval before entering service. EWS would take delivery of its first completed Class 67 in October 1999.

BELOW 58024 shunts a mixture of JXA, KEA and JUA box wagons at Newport Alexandra Dock Junction yard on 15 July 1997. Under EWS management, the '58s' strayed a long way from their East Midlands origins.

LEFT 90029 *Frachtverbindungen* passes Moore with 6G94, the 15.50 Carlisle to Bescot train, on 18 May 1998, in red DB livery which would take on greater significance a decade later. This was a former RfD service which became an integral part of the EWS Enterprise network.

The influx of new General Motors locomotives – the last of the 250 Class 66s would be delivered in June 2000 – heralded the almost total replacement of the EWS main-line diesel fleet within the space of a few years. First to go were the remaining '31s' and '33s', as well as the railfreight '47s' whose ranks had been swelled by the acquisition of RfD. The higher availability of the Class 66s meant that one new locomotive typically replaced three older machines. Soon the axe shifted to the relatively young Classes 58 and 56, which would be withdrawn from normal main-line use by 2002 and 2004 respectively. Many '58s' and '56s' would find further work on infrastructure projects in mainland Europe, as would some of EWS's redundant Class 37s.

The acquisition of RfD gave EWS its first electric locomotives, including a sizeable fleet of Class 92s which formed a common pool based at Crewe – even though some were owned by SNCF or European Passenger Services. The '92s' had been embarrassingly under-utilised since their introduction in 1993, partly because of a lack of traffic and partly because of difficulties in getting Railtrack certification for different routes in the UK. Under EWS management, a batch was modified to allow them to work on the West Coast main line for the first time. Clearance was gradually extended so that, by 2001, the whole of the active fleet was also passed to work on the East Coast main line, as well as on the dc routes between London and the Channel Tunnel and through the tunnel itself. But there was still not enough work to keep the class fully occupied and many examples were placed in store.

EWS's traction deployment policy was radically different from that of BR Trainload Freight or the three pre-privatisation TLF divisions. Pools for specific service groups or traffic types were abolished and EWS operated all locomotives on a common user basis. All 250 Class 66s formed a single pool based at Toton, which also had responsibility for Classes 58 and 60. This policy made it easier for EWS to adjust quickly to short-term fluctuations in traffic levels in different service groups.

As well as replacing many of its locomotives, EWS set about replenishing its wagon fleet.

EWS operational main line locomotive fleet, March 2001

Class 37	48
Class 47	42
Class 56	56
Class 58	21
Class 59	6
Class 60	99
Class 66	250
Class 67	29
Class 73	8
Class 86	10
Class 90	25
Class 92	46
Total	**640**

Since the early 1980s BR had required many of its customers to provide their own wagons, but Ed Burkhardt made it clear that this policy would be overturned. In the short term, EWS converted existing stock to cater for new traffic flows, notably MEA open-box wagons for coal and aggregates flows to locations without hopper discharge facilities. Some steel carriers and general purpose vans were brought back into commercial use after redeployment in railway engineering traffic. EWS also hired a number of wagon types from suppliers such as Tiphook and Cargowaggon, in order to cover new traffic flows at short notice.

To cater for longer-term needs, EWS formed a partnership with the US-based Thrall Car Company which set up a manufacturing plant in the former ABB works at York in summer 1997. A five-year deal promised a total of 2,500 wagons, although Burkhardt was keen to double that total and his Engineering Director, Jim Fisk, believed they could produce even more than that. About 85% of the wagons would be earmarked for new traffic. EWS opted for an American wagon builder because of the wide gulf in costs between US and European components, such as bogies. The US product would also have lower life-cycle maintenance costs. All wagons would be bogie designs, as they were better for track as well as providing a higher load capacity per unit length.

LEFT The boundaries between former Loadhaul, Transrail and Mainline Freight areas were soon forgotten as EWS redeployed its locomotives on a nationwide basis. Blue Circle Cement (later Lafarge) was one of the first customers to switch from EWS to Freightliner Heavy Haul. On 15 July 1998 ex-Loadhaul 56130 shunts PCA tanks at the Viewpark terminal after arriving as 6D38, the 12.27 from Oxwellmains.

Thrall Car wagon building programme

Date	Code	Type	Number series
1998	BYA	steel coil	966001 to 966260
1999	BRA	steel	964001 to 964050
1999	MBA	open box	500001 to 500300
1999	FAA	well wagon, intermodal	609001 to 609100
1999	FKA	low-deck intermodal twin set	81-70-4908-000-2 to 81-70-4908-149-7
2000	FCA	intermodal twin set	610001 to 610400
2001	HTA	coal hopper	310000 to 311161

The Thrall Car programme began with a 310-strong fleet of covered steel carriers, the first of which was formally handed over on 27 July 1998. The next priority was to expand the intermodal wagon fleet, for both domestic and international traffic. Three intermodal types were produced: a standard flat wagon, a low-deck flat wagon and a well wagon which would allow 'high cube' containers to be carried on many UK routes. Thrall Car then produced a fleet of 300 MBA 'gondola' bogie box wagons, suitable for coal, aggregates and any other load that could be discharged by mechanical grab. Finally, the largest single order with Thrall Car was for over 1,100 bogie coal hopper wagons, allowing the phasing out of the highly successful but dated two-axle merry-go-round hoppers.

ABOVE Many internationally registered vans found use on domestic flows of steel, paper and other packaged products. Several still carrying the anachronistic Ferrywagon brand are marshalled behind locomotive 56111 as it passes Whitchurch with 6M69, the 13.57 Cardiff Canton to Warrington Arpley trunk Enterprise train, on 1 September 1997.

Alongside the Thrall Car deal, EWS continued to use other wagon manufacturers for conversions such as the re-bodying of 250 redundant merry-go-round hoppers as MHA box wagons for infrastructure traffic, carried out by RFS at Doncaster, and the conversion of additional MEA wagons by Marcroft at Stoke-on-Trent. EWS also contracted a Slovakian builder to supply 20 Eurospine Piggyback wagon sets.

The investment in new locomotives and rolling stock was complemented by EWS's decision to create a national Customer Service Delivery Centre (CSDC). The purpose of the CSDC was to provide customers with a single point of contact for all service planning and delivery functions, 24 hours a day. Previously those functions had been carried out in different locations, using different

LEFT EWS Class 66s heralded a new era for railfreight traction. The first four '66s' to reach the UK – 66001/03/04/05 – form a convoy with 'heritage' locomotive D6603 as they pass Llanwern en route from Newport to Toton, on 20 August 1998. 66001 had been in the country since April, but 03/04/05 had only just been offloaded at Newport Docks.

systems and hardware, which resulted in a fragmented service.

A site at Doncaster was chosen for the 41,000sq ft CSDC building, which opened in stages from September 1998. Most of the CSDC's 320 staff worked in the vast Control Room, where some 180 workstations were optimally placed to allow verbal as well as electronic exchanges of information. Located at the centre of the Control Room was the Production Unit, with responsibility for the minute-by-minute delivery of train services. Large screens around the room displayed real-time updates on any major network disruption, such as the closure of a line by flooding.

Seven customer service teams – Royal Mail and Charter, Infrastructure, Metals/Petroleum, Minerals, Rail Services, Construction and Enterprise/Intermodal – were responsible for taking orders, planning resources and ensuring orders were correctly fulfilled. The Production Unit was organised geographically, with teams covering closely defined areas corresponding to those used by Railtrack. Within the Production Unit were two further control functions: Mobile Control, responsible for allocating traction and wagon resources; and Maintenance Control, overseeing the planned maintenance of locomotive and wagon fleets.

While the CSDC undoubtedly brought some customer benefits, persuading experienced production staff to move from all parts of the country to Doncaster proved stickier than anticipated. The result was a loss of crucial expertise. The overall effectiveness of the CSDC fell short of expectations and its functions were eventually scaled down.

While traffic volumes grew and new wagons rolled prolifically off the production line, EWS was shaken by the sudden and unexpected 'resignation' of its inspirational Chairman and Chief Executive on 8 July 1999. The news brought puzzlement, with the reasons emerging only gradually. Ed Burkhardt had been the victim of a culture clash between UK and American perspectives at boardroom level –he had a sharper understanding of the commercial realities of UK railfreight than the other US and New Zealand members – and had in fact been dismissed. Burkhardt had also provoked conflict at times with politicians and with Railtrack, who amongst other things had refused to endorse EWS's ambition to treble railfreight in ten years.

Initially Tom Power, co-founder of Wisconsin Central, took over as EWS Chief Executive until Philip Mengel was appointed to the role in January 2000. Indications of deep-seated problems became clear when Mengel wrote to his customers in the context of investment and traffic growth: 'Despite these achievements, EWS is not now providing

RIGHT Limestone is offloaded at Dewsbury from train 6G80, the 08.51 departure from Rylstone, on 9 April 1999. The train locomotive is 56106. This terminal was provided at minimal cost by using an existing siding with an adjacent area of spare land – just the kind of resourcefulness for which EWS became well known. While BR had moved away from providing terminal operations, EWS was keen to offer its customers as complete a package as possible.

ABOVE Even Class 08s found themselves on charter work from time to time. 08466 and 08651 provide top-and-tail traction for the Monmouthshire Railway Society 'Splott Pilot', as it passes Splott Junction in the Cardiff Docks complex on 2 October 1999. GAVIN MORRISON

service performance levels that are satisfactory to our customers or to us. Simply stated, the current level of train cancellations and service failures is not acceptable.' He went on to challenge his own staff: 'We must look inside EWS and recognise the urgent need to improve our business processes in such areas as train planning, driver rostering, ground operations and many others. We must rapidly become a true customer service delivery company, focused intently on customer requirements of responsiveness, reliability, timeliness and competitive cost.'

From summer 2000 EWS's comprehensive customer magazine, *EWS Focus*, was replaced by a slimmed-down publication pointedly entitled *Customer First*. Each month the back page of *Customer First* showed as a bar chart the percentage of trains cancelled by EWS – indicating willingness to grapple with an awkward but crucial issue.

Poor service performance had indeed begun to cost EWS dearly, as other railfreight operators ate into its traffic base. In its first three years, EWS had faced little real competition from within the railway industry: Direct Rail Services seemed interested only in its own niche market of nuclear materials, and the pioneering National Power open-access operation had sold out to EWS. But from 2000 onwards, customers seeking contracts for new or renewed business looked increasingly critically at EWS's track record and sometimes found a better offer elsewhere.

The first major challenge to EWS's near-monopoly of non-containerised freight was Railtrack's decision to place a share of its infrastructure train movements with Freightliner, who in due course took charge of the local distribution centre at Crewe Basford Hall yard. A smaller but still significant loss came in the form of Blue Circle shifting some (and eventually all) of its cement traffic to Freightliner. EWS had been involved in restoring the Weaste branch to use for a new cement flow, but was destined never to haul a train to that location.

Accusations of 'cherry-picking' levelled at companies competing with EWS were perhaps unfair – railfreight is, after all, an open market in which the real competition comes from the road haulier. But from an EWS perspective it must have been frustrating to see previously stable and profitable flows disappear, leaving the company with smaller-scale and in some cases marginal traffic flows.

The position of wagonload traffic was delicate. If a competitor took the main traffic flow on a particular Enterprise service – as happened with cement to the North of Scotland – then EWS would struggle to maintain that service for other, smaller traffic flows. Freightliner and GB Railfreight both proved formidable competitors in the lucrative coal market, leaving EWS with underused yards and other resources in some parts of the country. EWS counterattacked by entering the market for deep-sea containers, but the gains in that area were relatively small compared with the loss of coal, aggregates and various other bulk flows.

Further problems included the disruption to Channel Tunnel freight services caused by

EWS operational main-line locomotive fleet, March 2006

Class 37	9
Class 59	6
Class 60	73
Class 66	250
Class 67	28
Class 90	10
Class 92	35
Total	**411**

LEFT The construction sector is closely dependent on the national economy and the railway has to cope with its peaks and troughs. To handle an increase in aggregates traffic in the South East, EWS provided a small fleet of two-axle HGA hopper wagons, which started life as PGA aggregates wagons before having their sides cut down for infrastructure use as ZFA 'Gunnells'. 60045 *The Permanent Way Institution* passes Stratford with 34 HGAs forming 6V79, the 09.41 from Marks Tey to West Drayton, on 3 April 2002.

hundreds of asylum seekers in 2001, a strike threat in late 2002 and, in the context of potential new traffic flows, the withdrawal of government freight facilities grants in England in 2003. In any event, new flows became scarcer as EWS slimmed down its wagonload network – the name 'Enterprise' was gradually dropped – and concentrated on retaining high-volume trainload business.

Continuing traffic losses, including the untimely end of the Royal Mail contract in early 2004, forced EWS to shed more staff and reduce its locomotive fleet and maintenance facilities. Crewe diesel depot and Cardiff Canton faced the axe, as did smaller depots at Saltley, Leicester, Peterborough, Hither Green and Millerhill. Most of EWS's remaining Class 47s were declared surplus, along with further reductions in the Class 37 and Class 56 fleets.

At the end of 2003, EWS Chief Executive Philip Mengel was replaced by Keith Heller, previously a director of the Canadian National railway company which acquired Wisconsin Central – and therefore a controlling interest in EWS – in 2001. The new CEO carried forward the policies of his predecessor, eager to transform EWS into 'the low cost operator of choice in the UK'. More locomotives were withdrawn or stored and more depot and yard facilities shut down in a drive to control costs. By March 2006, EWS had just 411 main-line locomotives in active service, as shown in the table below. This was by no means the end of the cutbacks.

While EWS faced ever stiffer competition in the UK, in 2005 it founded an entirely new venture to provide a launch pad in mainland Europe. Although little information has been published about Euro Cargo Rail – EWS largely closed its doors to the press in the first years of the 21st century – it was an astonishing success, competing with SNCF to build up a varied traffic base in many regions of France and capturing an estimated 12% of the French railfreight market by early 2010. As well as using 60 EWS Class 66s exported from the UK, Euro Cargo Rail acquired a sizeable fleet of locomotives built by Vossloh and Bombardier. This was strictly a mainland European operation, not to be confused with the dwindling tonnage of railfreight using the Channel Tunnel.

At home, EWS broadened its business base by launching Axiom Rail, a supplier of rolling stock maintenance, refurbishment, leasing and suspension systems to the European market. EWS also acquired the well-established wagon builder and repairer Marcroft, a step which required the approval of the Competition Commission because of a perceived threat to free competition in the railway industry.

In 2006, Keith Heller reintroduced the concept of business divisions to EWS, with separate teams for Construction, Energy, Industrial and Network. The similarity to the subsectors of Trainload Freight days was striking, with each team carrying responsibility

RIGHT The Customer Service Delivery Centre at Doncaster employed nearly 400 people, combining the functions of service planning and delivery which used to be spread across the regions. The vast Control Room, seen here on 25 July 2000, measured 197ft by 131ft.

not only for the delivery of train services but also for its own financial performance. But there were some differences, too. The Industrial team covered metals and petroleum traffic, volumes of petroleum having declined sharply since the 1990s, while Network dealt with a wide range of operations including infrastructure, automotive and intermodal traffic. Locomotives were allotted to specific segments, but only for however long it took for them to complete a sequence of journeys; there was no return to the fixed resource dedication of Trainload Freight days.

Signs of a recovery in EWS's health included several successful bids to win bulk freight flows back from competitors and, in 2009, the promise of a limited return of mail traffic on the West Coast main line. Channel Tunnel traffic remained an embarrassment, however, although Heller presided over the introduction of temperature-controlled trains between Spain and London a few months before he retired as CEO in January 2010.

Meanwhile, EWS itself changed hands, becoming part of the pan-European logistics company DB Schenker in 2007. Outward signs of the takeover were few, with a full launch of the Schenker brand not taking place until 2009. Even then, only a token selection of locomotives would initially receive DB's bright red livery. The name and colours of EWS would live on as a reminder of Ed Burkhardt's ambitious – albeit not entirely fulfilled – vision for railfreight in the 1990s.

ABOVE EWS Class 47s appeared on GNER trains when they were diverted away from the electrified network due to engineering work. 47785 *Fiona Castle* waits at Leeds with the 10.40 departure to London King's Cross on 12 March 2000. The train would follow a circuitous route via Normanton and Knottingley before regaining the East Coast main line at Shaftholme Junction. GAVIN MORRISON

RIGHT 33030 rests at Aberdeen Guild Street freight depot on 31 May 2000. The use of Class 33 traction for shunting and trip duties at Aberdeen was a surprising move, a long way from their Southern Region home territory. GAVIN MORRISON

ABOVE EWS inherited the bulk of BR's railfreight infrastructure, including a number of large and under-utilised marshalling yards. Long-stored wagons fill most of the sidings at Tees Yard on 1 June 2007, as 66088 arrives with the 6N32 lime empties from Lackenby. It will couple up to a rake of HGAs from Redcar and depart as train 6M46 to Hardendale.

ABOVE 66054 heads south from Normanton with 4O52, the 18.29 from Wakefield to Southampton Docks, on 9 June 2008. One of EWS's smartest moves was developing its intermodal strategy to include deep-sea traffic, in direct competition with Freightliner.

BELOW EWS Class 90s were a useful asset for hire to passenger companies, although they saw minimal use on freight. 90023 is on hire to Silverlink as it waits at London Euston with the 17.22 'Cobbler' service to Northampton on 10 June 2005. HUGH BALLANTYNE

RIGHT EWS avoided the cost of repaints by applying vinyls to older liveries, including the Trainload Freight two-tone grey scheme. 60034 *Carnedd Llewelyn* arrives at Peak Forest with 6M17, the 10.18 empties from Leeds Stourton, on 10 April 2006.

ABOVE Having been made redundant from mail traffic, some Class 67s were used on Enterprise trip workings, usually singly but occasionally in pairs. 67014 and 67021 pass Hoghton with 6F42, the 11.48 Blackburn to Warrington Arpley trip, on 2 April 2007. The train on this occasion included empty steel carriers returning to Hull, as well as empty vans for mainland Europe.

LEFT 08523 manoeuvres the last rake of empty wagons at the Albion plant at Sandbach on 14 February 2007, while 66100 waits to haul them offsite as train 6F17 to Warrington Arpley.While EWS talked hopefully of a possible recovery in chemicals traffic, in reality the business declined relentlessly as customers changed their manufacturing and distribution policies.

four

Coal

The running down of deep mining in the UK was already well advanced by the time EWS was formed. Just 25 pits were still winding coal at the end of 1996, including five which formed part of the Selby complex with its high-output loading facility at Gascoigne Wood. Opencast coal was thriving, especially in South Wales – where no rail-connected deep mines remained in operation – and Scotland, where the only deep mine, Longannet, was linked to the adjacent power station by a conveyor belt. The coal import terminals at Liverpool, Avonmouth and Immingham were up and running, but the overall tonnage of imported coal burned by UK power generators was still modest.

LEFT The Scottish opencast revival lasted into the 21st century, with several Ayrshire terminals sending coal to English and Scottish power stations. 66216 runs round its train of merry-go-round wagons at Chalmerston on 27 August 2003, after working 6R72, the 14.35 departure from Falkland Junction yard.

In addition to the power station traffic, EWS handled numerous flows of coal for industrial and domestic customers. These ranged from well-established, high-volume deliveries of imported coal for British Steel Llanwern and Scunthorpe to smaller movements of domestic coal to regional distribution depots – a market which was declining sharply, but which still generated a weekly trainload from Gascoigne Wood to Scotland using former Cawoods containers. The Transrail Enterprise network had enabled household deliveries to resume to several coal concentration depots, including Gobowen, Blackburn and Carlisle.

In the mid-1990s the railway gained several new flows of coal to cement works. EWS won further traffic of this type, with deliveries starting to Penyffordd (Padeswood) in July 1996 and Clitheroe, Rugby (for New Bilton) and Tavistock Junction (for Plymstock) by the end of 1997. The Rugby and Tavistock Junction flows involved final delivery by road. EWS was able to adapt to frequent changes in the source of supply, such as when Clitheroe took coal from Maltby, Redcar and Killoch in the last few months of 1997. Unfortunately, the Tavistock Junction traffic ceased in 1999 when Plymstock works closed.

The former British Steel deep-water import terminal at Hunterston was too good to remain idle after the closure of Ravenscraig steelworks in 1992. It returned to use in January 1997, with EWS initially hauling trainloads of imported coal to Scottish and English power stations. Other ports which started loading coal on to rail in the late 1990s included Redcar, Hull, New Holland, Grain (Thamesport) and Newport. Trial flows of imported coal ran to Slough for Slough Estates, to Acton for Guinness, and to Ipswich and Norwich for British Sugar.

EWS's takeover of the National Power (NP) open-access rail operation, in April 1998, reinforced the company's position as the major haulier of bulk railfreight. NP's rail assets included a total of 106 hopper wagons, six Class 59 locomotives, a maintenance depot at Ferrybridge, one depot shunter and some 50 staff. The takeover gave EWS its first taste of bogie coal hopper wagons and its first ownership of General Motors traction. Initially the ex-NP Class 59s and wagons remained in use on their Aire Valley home ground, but they would later find work elsewhere, including a lengthy spell on the Liverpool to Fiddlers Ferry circuit.

While some of the UK's older coal-fired power stations were facing closure because of new emissions regulations, the mothballed Uskmouth station was reopened by AES Electric as Fifoots Point in early 2000. A 2½-mile stretch of the Uskmouth branch was reinstated to allow coal to be delivered to the site for the first time since 1984. EWS won the contract to supply Fifoots Point with imported coal from Newport Docks and home-produced coal from Parc Slip. The new rail facilities at Fifoots Point included a bottom-discharge facility for HAA-type merry-go-round wagons, as well as terminals for incoming lime and outgoing ash. Operations at Fifoots Point ceased in 2002 when its owner went into receivership, but the power station would later reopen under its original name of Uskmouth.

Other developments in South Wales included the closure of Coedbach washery in 1998 and Gwaun-cae-Gurwen in 1999. Coal traffic from Cwmbargoed ceased, pending the outcome of a

BELOW Although Liverpool Bulk Terminal was built with coal to Fiddlers Ferry power station in mind, it handled other traffic flows as required. Nearly-new locomotive 66014 draws its train of MEA box wagons through the loading point at Liverpool on 1 June 1999 before forming 6P82, the14.30 departure to Clitheroe.

ABOVE 37412 *Driver John Elliot* passes Duffryn on 16 July 1997, with the 6E07, the 16.28 Coedbach to Immingham train, conveying containerised anthracite duff for the manufacture of smokeless briquettes. This traffic later switched to merry-go-round wagons after hopper discharge facilities had been installed at Immingham.

planning inquiry into the Ffos-y-Fran reclamation scheme. In 1998, EWS gained a new short-term flow of reclaimed coal from Brynteg by establishing a lineside loading pad on the Onllwyn branch, with no need for a siding or any other infrastructure work. As for destinations, Aberthaw power station remained a major consumer of both home-produced and imported coal, but the closure of the British Steel blast furnaces at Llanwern in 2002 brought an end to the intensive Port Talbot to Llanwern coal flow.

One decisive step towards the demise of the merry-go-round coal wagon – surely one of the railfreight icons of the 20th century – was EWS's decision in early 2000 to introduce a new design of bogie coal-hopper wagon. The company used its experience with the ex-NP wagons to determine the best body profile for maximising carrying capacity and ensuring efficient discharge. An initial order for 280 wagons from the Thrall factory in York was soon extended to a total of 845 vehicles, the first of which would be delivered in December 2000.

Classified as 'HTA', the new coal hoppers would have a capacity of 76 tonnes, roughly double that of a two-axle merry-go-round wagon, and a gross laden weight of 102 tonnes, the maximum allowed for a bogie wagon on the Railtrack network. The HTAs would be able to travel at 75mph empty and 60mph loaded, compared with 60mph empty and 45mph loaded for most merry-go-round stock, a factor which would make pathing easier on busy main lines. Unlike merry-go-round stock, the HTAs would not be fitted with automatic hopper door operation, as this feature was not required by all customers.

The first HTAs entered normal revenue-earning service in January 2001. They became established on various routes including Avonmouth to Didcot, Hull to Ferrybridge, and Maltby to Drax, normally operating in 19-wagon rakes. This gave a train payload of more than 1,400 tonnes, an increase of more than a third on a typical merry-go-round train. The HTAs also started to appear on Anglo-Scottish trains in 2002 and on the intensive Immingham to Scunthorpe circuit in 2003. The order for HTA production was increased to a total of 1,145 wagons in 2002, bringing the Thrall Car wagon-building programme to a conclusion.

While EWS was equipping itself with second-generation air-braked coal wagons, it faced its first real competition from another railfreight operator. Freightliner Heavy Haul secured a contract with Enron to deliver coal to Aire Valley power stations in 2000, taking delivery of rolling stock which was similar to the HTA. The reality of the free market had struck home; not only would Freightliner increase its share of coal traffic substantially over the coming years, but further competition would come from operators including GB Railfreight in 2006 and Fastline Freight in 2008.

Imported coal continued to increase its dominance of the UK market. In most cases this meant longer journeys and therefore a higher tonne-mileage for the railway, even if less coal was being consumed. The challenge for the railway was to match its infrastructure and handling facilities with the traffic available, as it sometimes proved difficult to predict traffic trends accurately. The rising demand in England

Colliery closures, 1996-2008

1996	
Point of Ayr	North Wales
Markham Main	Yorkshire
Hem Heath	Staffordshire
Coventry	West Midlands
1997	
Bilsthorpe	Nottinghamshire
Asfordby	Leicestershire
1998	
Monktonhall	Lothian
Whitemoor (1)	Yorkshire
Silverdale	Staffordshire
1999	
North Selby (1)	Yorkshire
Calverton	Nottinghamshire
2000	
Annesley/Bentinck	Nottinghamshire
2002	
Longannet	Fife/Stirling
Prince of Wales	Yorkshire
2003	
Clipstone	Nottinghamshire
Betws (2)	South Wales
2004	
Riccall (1)	Yorkshire
Stillingfleet (1)	Yorkshire
Wistow (1)	Yorkshire
2005	
Ellington	North East
2006	
Rossington	Yorkshire
Harworth	Nottinghamshire
2008	
Tower	South Wales

(1) loaded at Gascoigne Wood
(2) not rail served

for Scottish opencast coal and imports from Hunterston prompted infrastructure improvements on the Settle to Carlisle line, but the tonnages actually carried over that line fluctuated considerably. On Merseyside a long-running campaign to reinstate the Olive Mount curve, simplifying train movements to and from Liverpool Docks, finally came to fruition in late 2008, but by then coal movements were running well below expectations and most other traffic flows to and from the docks had ceased.

Meanwhile, Immingham had strengthened its position as the number one port for foreign coal and the railway was constantly under pressure to provide facilities. By 2001, loading was taking place at four separate locations in the Immingham Dock complex; in the following year, the first stage of Humber International Terminal (HIT) was completed, with a capacity to offload coal from 100,000-tonne vessels. Immingham dispatched its thousandth coal train in 2003 and a further extension to HIT was authorised in 2005.

The output from the UK's deep mines continued to decline, as seams became worked out or too expensive to exploit. It was not only the old, established mines that closed; the 'super pit' at Asfordby in Leicestershire never achieved its potential and shut in 1997, while the Selby coalfield loading point at Gascoigne Wood dispatched its last train in November 2004.

In South West Scotland, opencast developments included new loading points

ABOVE 56060 passes the site of Frodingham motive power depot at Scunthorpe with a loaded train from Immingham, on 3 June 1999. In the background is an empty Greater Manchester refuse train coming off the Roxby branch. Despite covering a distance of just 22 miles, the flow of imported coal from Immingham to Scunthorpe was a valuable high-volume business for EWS.

Coal loading points, December 2008

Immingham	import terminal
Hull	import terminal
Redcar	import terminal
Tyne Dock	import terminal
North Blyth	import terminal
Leith	import terminal
Hunterston	import terminal
Liverpool	import terminal
Ellesmere Port	import terminal
Newport	import terminal
Avonmouth	import terminal
Portbury	import terminal
Daw Mill	colliery
Thoresby	colliery
Welbeck	colliery
Maltby	colliery
Kellingley	colliery
Hatfield	colliery
Butterwell	opencast loading
Widdrington	opencast loading
Ravenstruther	opencast loading
Mossend	opencast loading
Killoch	opencast loading
Chalmerston	opencast loading
Greenburn	opencast loading
New Cumnock	opencast loading
Onllwyn	opencast and washery
Gwaun-cae-Gurwen	opencast loading
Cwmbargoed	opencast loading
Tower	railhead for Aberpergwm

ABOVE Class 58s were built for coal and that is how some of them spent their final years, operating mainly in the East Midlands. 58047 approaches Stenson Junction with 6P46, the 10.45 Drakelow to Toton merry-go-round train, on 16 June 2000.

at New Cumnock in 1999 and Greenburn in 2004, supplementing the existing flows from Chalmerston, Killoch and Knockshinnoch. The Scottish opencast market was closely contested by EWS and Freightliner Heavy Haul. North of the Forth estuary, the closure of Longannet colliery in 2002 created a demand for more rail movements to Longannet power station: from May 2004, EWS would be contracted to run 12 merry-go-round trains each weekday from Hunterston to Longannet. Initially these comprised 30 merry-go-round wagons, which was very short by 21st century standards, but they were later increased to 38. The Forth Bridge was unable to accommodate EWS's new HTA wagons (or any other bogie coal hoppers for that matter), but after the Stirling-Alloa-Kincardine line reopened in 2008 the situation changed, with EWS losing no time in introducing HTAs on the rerouted Longannet trains.

EWS was always keen to maximise train tonnages as a means of increasing revenue without incurring extra train-crew and pathing costs. Already the use of HTA wagons made it possible to carry a higher tonnage within a given train length, but in 2006, EWS experimented with double-headed 'jumbo' trains comprising 42 HTAs between Carlisle and Yorkshire, splitting into two 21-wagon portions for final delivery to Aire Valley power stations. While on the main line the 'jumbos' performed well, but the need to split them into portions at both ends of the route because of limited capacity at terminals lessened their overall effectiveness.

In the industrial and domestic market, EWS continued to supply coal to major users such as Corus (formerly British Steel) and the cement manufacturers, but the smaller flows withered away. Exports of containerised coal for Northern Ireland via Liverpool Seaforth finished in 2004, and the Coalite plant at Bolsover – which once generated inward and outward traffic – closed in the same year. The closure of Gobowen coal depot in 2004 marked the end of domestic coal traffic in HEA hopper wagons. After this the surviving HEAs would be allocated to the Redcar to Scunthorpe coke flow, which would continue until 2008.

In late 2008, coal still accounted for 47% of railfreight lifted (i.e. tonnage) and 40% of railfreight moved (i.e. weight and distance combined) in the UK. EWS was still the overall market leader among the railfreight companies, but Freightliner Heavy Haul held a sizeable chunk of the Anglo-Scottish traffic, as well as flows from English ports and collieries to Fiddlers Ferry and the Aire and Trent valleys. GB Railfreight was particularly active in Yorkshire and the North East. Fastline had recently started its own coal operation, but its parent company would soon face bankruptcy. Within EWS, the transition from two-axle merry-go-round wagons to HTAs was almost complete, with just four flows hanging on with two-axle stock: Newport to Uskmouth, New Cumnock to Hope, Mossend to Drax, and Mossend to West Burton.

ABOVE 56089 leaves Healey Mills yard on 25 August 2000 with 6Z51, the 12.30 departure to Immingham, comprising PFA wagons with empty containers for loading at the CPL briquetting works. Cawoods containers carried coal for export to Ireland from various loading points to Ellesmere Port and, later, Seaforth.

RIGHT The reopening of Uskmouth power station as Fifoots Point brought a revival of coal traffic to the Newport area. The discharge facility at the power station was built to handle traditional merry-go-round wagons, even though they were soon to be replaced by the new generation of HTA stock. 66046 arrives at Fifoots Point with train 6Z91 from East Usk Junction, on 25 October 2000.

UK coal production and imports, million tonnes

	1996	2008
Deep mined	32.2	8.1
Opencast	18.0	10.0
Coal imports	17.8	43.9
Total	**68.0**	**62.0**

ABOVE EWS used its two-axle MEA wagons to deliver coal to several industrial destinations without hopper discharge facilities. 60017 approaches Helsby with 6Z52, the 12.05 from Liverpool Bulk Terminal to Penyffordd, on 27 March 2002.

RIGHT 60081 was repainted in Great Western Railway green livery and renamed *Isambard Kingdom Brunel* in 2000. It is pictured passing the site of Warrington Bank Quay low-level station on 1 September 2003, in charge of 6F89, the 10.21 from Fiddlers Ferry to Liverpool Bulk Terminal. The wagons are ex-National Power JMA hoppers.

ABOVE 66168 heads north at Arten Gill with 6S89, the 14.02 Milford to Falkland Junction empties, on 8 September 2004. Both Milford and Falkland Junction were staging points; the wagons would have originated at Drax or Eggborough and were destined for reloading at one of the Scottish opencast sites. The promise of increased coal traffic justified significant track and signalling upgrades for the Settle to Carlisle line.

LEFT 66182 passes Barnetby with 4Y80, the 09.10 Eggborough to Immingham empties, on 16 June 2003, while Freightliner loco 66524 waits to couple up to its train in the adjacent sidings. Immingham became the busiest of the rail-served coal import terminals, but EWS would face competition from Freightliner, GB Railfreight and, for a time, Fastline Freight in transporting the coal to power stations.

five

Metals

EWS's metals portfolio in 1996 was dominated by British Steel plc, whose 'big four' integrated steelworks at Port Talbot, Llanwern, Scunthorpe and Teesside (Redcar and Lackenby) generated huge volumes of steady trainload traffic. It was just the kind of business for which the railway was ideally suited.

LEFT 37688 passes Milford South Junction with eight BDA wagons forming 6M02, the 14.36 Lynemouth to Wolverhampton aluminium billet train, on 7 August 1998. The billet was destined for Rogerstone in South Wales, which at that time was transported from Wolverhampton to Rogerstone by road, providing a backload for lorries delivering steel from South Wales to the West Midlands.

RIGHT With Humber and Lindsey refineries visible in the background, 60067 *James Clerk-Maxwell* approaches its destination with 6K25, the 14.42 Scunthorpe to Immingham iron ore empties, on 29 October 1997.

In South Wales, EWS carried imported iron ore from Port Talbot to Llanwern in seven daily 3,000-tonne trainloads. From early 1997, this traffic utilised a pool of three locomotives: one EWS Class 60 and two Class 59s on hire from Mendip Rail. Other raw materials transported to the South Wales plants by rail included coal from Port Talbot to Llanwern, lime from Hardendale to Port Talbot, scrap metal from Shotton to Port Talbot and slab from Teesside to Port Talbot.

In the outward direction, the South Wales plants generated interworks flows of hot rolled coil to Ebbw Vale, Trostre and Shotton, as well as trainload deliveries to Round Oak for distribution to customers in the West Midlands. Further destinations for South Wales coil included Orb (Uskmouth branch) and Goole. The British Steel tinplate works at Ebbw Vale and Trostre generated vanloads of tinplate for Worcester and Wisbech, conveyed respectively by the Round Oak steel train and the Enterprise network.

British Steel Scunthorpe received its supplies of iron ore and coal from Immingham, in much the same way as Llanwern was supplied from Port Talbot. Outward traffic from Scunthorpe included slab to Teesside and billet to distribution terminals at Rotherham and Wolverhampton. The Teesside complex generated a wide variety of railfreight traffic: EWS ran a daily train from Hardendale quarry to Teesside, conveying limestone for Redcar and lime for Lackenby, as well as block loads of hot rolled coil from Lackenby, to Corby, Dalzell, Wakefield and Blackburn, and slab from Lackenby to Shelton, Workington and Port Talbot. The British Steel sections mill at Shelton produced trainloads of finished product to Middlesbrough for export.

The Allied Steel & Wire complex at Cardiff was a long-standing user of rail. It received trainloads of scrap metal from Exeter, Willesden and several terminals in the West Midlands, plus a combined train of imported billet from Hamworthy and scrap from Swindon. (The Hamworthy train also carried finished reinforcing rods from Cardiff to Southampton.) EWS used a combination of block trains and the Enterprise wagonload network to carry wire rod in coil and reinforcing rods from Cardiff to Purfleet, Burton-on-Trent, Wakefield, Warrington and Mossend.

LEFT 60063 arrives at Dalzell with 6S58, the 01.06 departure from Lackenby, on 15 July 1998. After the closure of Ravenscraig, the steel industry generated little railfreight in Scotland apart from regular movements of slab from Teesside to Dalzell plate mill.

LEFT 09105 shunts BYA wagons at Newport Docks on 26 October 2000. For a time the enhanced handling facilities at Newport were busy with imports and exports of steel coil.

The CoSteel works at Sheerness used EWS for its inward deliveries of scrap metal from Willesden and Snailwell, plus some outward wagonloads of finished product which Transrail had won back to rail thanks to the Enterprise network. Another destination for rail-borne scrap metal was the United Engineering Steels (UES) plant at Aldwarke, which received trains from Stockton, Shipley and several terminals in the Midlands. A short-distance feeder service ran between Aldwarke and UES's Stocksbridge plant, conveying a share of the scrap traffic as well as semi-finished product.

The formerly complex web of steel trains in the Sheffield area had been much reduced by the time EWS was formed. However, the remnants of Tinsley yard were still used for carrying semi-finished steel to and from the Avesta plant at Tinsley, with regular flows to and from Grimsby and to Liverpool Seaforth.

While EWS inherited a profitable baseload of trainload steel traffic, its new commercial team led by Neil Crossland identified many opportunities for expansion, some following the trainload model and others using the fast-growing Enterprise wagonload network. In Trainload Freight days, BR had concentrated on maximising train tonnages on specific routes and had lost most of its flows of finished products – such as cold reduced coil or 'bright steel' – to regional distribution terminals. Even in the West Midlands, with its large concentration of engineering firms consuming steel from South Wales and the North East, BR had closed all but one of its steel railheads, leaving only Wolverhampton which had a reduced service. The privately operated, covered steel terminal at Round Oak had also faced the threat of closure.

EWS lost little time in increasing its share of finished and semi-finished steel to the West Midlands, using its newly delivered Thrall Car covered coil wagons as well as existing stock. Loadhaul had begun investing in improved handling facilities at Wolverhampton and EWS authorised the spending of a further £1.8 million on the site, more than doubling the size of the warehouse and providing a second 35tonne gantry crane. The throughput at Wolverhampton increased from just two trains a day in 1994 to between seven and nine in 1998. The Round Oak railhead similarly gained a new lease of life, with up to four trains a day operating by 1998. Brierley Hill steel terminal was reopened for CoSteel traffic from Sheerness and a new overflow railhead was provided at Walsall Tasker Street.

Britain's ports offered great potential for new or increased steel traffic. One of the first successes was Immingham, where the opening of the Nordic terminal in February 1997 enabled the start of several new flows as well as an increase in Avesta traffic from 180,000 to 500,000 tonnes annually. The efficiency of the Avesta traffic was to improve further in 2001, when EWS introduced a fleet of BVA wagons that could carry both exports of slab from Tinsley to Immingham and return imports of coil from Immingham to Tinsley.

Across the Humber estuary, in autumn 1997 the port of Hull benefited from the country's first covered transhipment berth for transferring

RIGHT 56095 departs from Seaforth container terminal with 6E14, the 10.50 train to Tinsley, on 9 August 2001. The inward working of this service conveyed stainless steel from the Avesta plant at Tinsley for export to the USA.

ABOVE 60066 *John Logie Baird* passes Washwood Heath on 23 February 2001 with 6Z42, the 02.11 Margam to Corby train. Corby tube works switched its source of supply from Teesside to South Wales when the Lackenby (Teesside) plant stopped producing coil.

steel between a ship and railway wagons, built at a cost to ABP of some £3.4 million. Various short-term and trial flows ran to and from Hull in 1998, including exports of coil from Shotton, pipes from Stanton and aluminium billet from Lynemouth, and imports of coil to Glasgow, pipes to Hartlepool and rail to Baileyfield. The port of Goole had already had its rail connection restored to use by Loadhaul, and EWS further developed the facility with a daily feeder service to and from Rotherham.

The port of Boston made a high-profile return to the railway network when the first trainload of imported steel coil left the refurbished sidings in October 1997. A £2.2 million government grant enabled this revival after a gap of nearly four years. By the end of 1998 a twice-weekly service was operating from Boston to Round Oak, conveying steel for distribution in the West Midlands. Other East Coast ports which began handling steel traffic by rail again included Ipswich – used for exports of pipes from Hartlepool and steel billet from Allied Steel & Wire at Cardiff during 1997/98 – and Purfleet, the destination of a thrice-weekly trainload of billet from Cardiff in 1998. South of the Thames, the Victa Rail terminal at Hoo Junction overcame the lack of a rail connection to the port of Northfleet by handling regular volumes of imported coil to Wolverhampton.

On the west side of the country, ABP opened a £2.5 million railhead in Newport docks for exports and imports of steel in early 1998. At the port of Liverpool, European Metals Recycling (EMR) invested the relatively modest sum of £250,000 in new rail handling facilities so that it could receive trainloads of scrap from various locations. EMR later received government funding to help improve its rail terminal, while EWS showed flexibility by running scrap trains from unusual locations including St Erth, in the far west of Cornwall, and Pickering, on the North Yorkshire Moors Railway.

EWS gained additional steel traffic to Liverpool in 2000, when the port authority opened a £3 million terminal for handling exports of cold reduced coil. The first train to the new terminal ran from Lackenby and a regular Enterprise connection was later established for coil from Shotton and the South Wales plants.

Steel pipe traffic was not new to the railway, but under EWS management the number of fixed-term contracts to carry pipes for export and domestic use increased markedly. Alongside a regular wagonload flow of pipes from British Steel Hartlepool to Laurencekirk for the North Sea oil industry, EWS won a series of block train movements from Hartlepool to Georgemas Junction – a distance of 500 miles. A 1998 contract with Transco required trainload movements of coated pipes

LEFT The British Steel (later Corus) rail mill at Workington received a daily trainload of steel bloom from Teesside. A rake of BBA wagons awaits unloading in the bloom shed at Workington on 30 August 2002.

from the British Pipe Coaters factory at Leith to temporary railheads at Bamber Bridge, Grantham and Yarwell (Nene Valley Railway). Export traffic included trains from Hartlepool to Teesport, Hartlepool to Ipswich, and Leith to Immingham. EWS's interest in pipe traffic was underlined by the provision of 30 BTA pipe-carrying wagons in 1997 by fitting sturdy stanchions to existing steel carriers.

The pipe manufacturer Stanton returned to rail in 1996. The initial traffic included a succession of trains from Stanton to Plymouth for South West Water, followed by movements to Immingham (for export to Peru), St Blazey (for a drainage project on Bodmin Moor), Redmire (for Yorkshire Water) and Hoo Junction (for the building of the Millennium Dome).

It was bad news for EWS when Corus (formed in 1999 through the merger of British Steel and Dutch steel producer Koninklijke Hoogovens) closed Shelton steelworks, near Stoke-on-Trent. The closure took place in summer 2000 and caused the demise of two trainload flows: slab from Teesside to Shelton and finished sections from Shelton to Middlesbrough. Small compensation for this closure came in the form of a new flow of sections from Teesside for export through Mostyn Docks.

Corus announced a much bigger round of cutbacks in the following year, which deprived EWS of a number of longstanding, high-volume freight flows. Ebbw Vale tinplate works closed completely, bringing an end to inward flows of coil and outward tinplate and leaving the Ebbw Vale branch without regular freight traffic. Primary steelmaking at Llanwern ceased, which led to the loss of intensive iron ore and coal trains from Port Talbot. The Teesside complex stopped producing hot rolled coil, which meant that, from 2002, Corby tube works received its coil from South Wales instead of Lackenby. There were some small gains, too: Llanwern started receiving trainloads of slab from Teesside, while Hartlepool tube works had to be supplied with coil from South Wales instead of Teesside, resulting in more tonne-miles for EWS.

EWS boosted its share of export traffic from Scunthorpe in July 2002 by introducing intermodal trains to various ports (including Felixstowe, Thamesport and Immingham), conveying wire rod in coil in ISO containers for export to South East Asia. The business grew rapidly and EWS celebrated its 100th train in December 2003.

Another EWS innovation was the introduction of 86 20ft containers for domestic flows of small steel coils, enabling the company to break into a market sector previously dominated by road transport. The containers entered service in 2002, carried on FCA wagons and put to use on flows from South Wales to Round Oak and Middlesbrough.

The collapse of Allied Steel & Wire in 2002 brought an abrupt (albeit temporary) end to

RIGHT The Nordic terminal at Immingham provided covered accommodation for shipments of moisture-sensitive, cold-reduced coil. A rake of BIA and BXA wagons is pictured during unloading on 7 August 2002.

RIGHT 60052 passes Willington with 6V40, the 06.02 Lackenby to Llanwern slab train, on 17 October 2003. This long-distance flow enabled Corus to match overproduction at Lackenby with increased demand for slab in South Wales.

flows of wire rod in coil and reinforcing bar from Cardiff and Sheerness. This was doubtless a contributory factor in the closure of the Cobra distribution terminal at Wakefield in early 2003. Both Cardiff and Sheerness steel plants were revived under new ownership, but outward traffic was slow to return. The Cardiff plant supplied materials for construction work at Heathrow Airport in late 2003, with flows to Burton-on-Trent and Rotherham following in 2004.

Further rationalisation by Corus was announced in 2005, this time targeting its rail production operations at Workington and Castleton. Both sites closed completely, with Corus investing £130 million in a replacement casting mill and rail production facility at Scunthorpe. The new plant would be able to produce 120-metre lengths of rail, compared with a maximum of just 40 metres at Workington. The Workington plant received its last trainload of slabs in August 2006, heralding the end of some 129 years of steel production at the Cumbrian site. (It was, however, not quite the end of the story. Delays in the commissioning of the Scunthorpe plant meant that Workington continued to weld rail lengths imported from France until 2007.)

A new flow of finished steel began in 2005, when EWS opened a distribution terminal at Bristol East on the site of the long-abandoned Freightliner depot. The terminal handled sections from Lackenby and Scunthorpe, conveyed by trunk metals trains from the North East to Newport Alexandra Dock Junction (ADJ) yard, and then by a trip working from ADJ to Bristol. A second new metals service from ADJ began operating in 2007, delivering imported cold reduced coil to Swindon for BMW Pressings.

For the best part of a decade, EWS had faced relatively little competition for metals traffic from other railfreight operators – perhaps because many of the wagons that carried steel products were owned by EWS. One of the first challenges came from Freightliner Heavy Haul who, in 2006, started running the Beeston to Cardiff scrap metal train using the JNA wagons previously stored at Long Marston. However, Freightliner could not make that traffic pay and it reverted to EWS in the following year.

Further challenges to EWS's monopoly of steel traffic came from the short-lived freight company Advenza, which carried scrap from several loading points to Cardiff in 2008, and from Colas Rail, which started hauling imported steel to the West Midlands in 2009. EWS, meanwhile, reverted to a policy redolent of Trainload Freight days: many of the smaller-scale flows such as steel sections to Bristol and Mostyn faced the axe, leaving the country's biggest railfreight operator to concentrate on the high-volume core business of moving raw materials and semi-finished products.

LEFT 37174 waits at North Blyth while its train is loaded on 16 July 2003. The Alcan import terminal at North Blyth generated trainloads of alumina to Lynemouth and Fort William, both using two-axle PCA tank wagons.

BJM
66038

ABOVE 66189 approaches Stainforth & Hatfield with 6M99, the 16.26 Immingham to Wolverhampton train, on 15 July 2008. The load is mainly imported steel coil for Wolverhampton Steel Terminal, but the first wagon is carrying gas oil and will be detached from the train at Bescot.

RIGHT A new freight terminal was provided in the up yard at Hitchin for incoming roadstone and outgoing scrap metal – served by Freightliner, Advenza and Direct Rail Services, as well as by EWS. 66021 waits to set back with its loaded JNA wagons on 28 August 2008, before departing as 6Z66, the 16.50 from Hitchin to Sheerness.

LEFT The rail connection to Laisterdyke scrapyard was reactivated for traffic to Port Talbot. As the yard had no run-round facility, trains entered the siding locomotive-first and reversed out onto the headshunt after loading. 66038 performs the reversing movement on 17 July 2006, while running as 6G99, the 16.29 from Laisterdyke to Healey Mills.

six

Petroleum and Chemicals

Having peaked at more than 20 million tonnes a year in the early 1970s, rail-borne petroleum traffic had declined to around seven million tonnes by the time EWS came on the scene. The factors contributing to decline included the building of pipelines, decrease in demand for products such as heavy fuel oil, exchange deals between producers and a gradual trend away from regional distribution depots, in favour of direct deliveries from refinery to customer. The imposition of emissions controls also forced the closure of some smaller terminals, where the cost of installing vapour recovery equipment would have been prohibitive. The terminals with the best prospects were those located a long way from the nearest refinery and with the capacity to handle 2,000-tonne-plus trainloads, such as Westerleigh, Kingsbury and Colwick.

Lindsey and Humber refineries at Immingham provided the largest concentration of petroleum traffic in 1996, and would continue to do so into the 21st century. The introduction of the Class 60s had enabled BR to increase train lengths on key flows to locations such as Kingsbury and Colwick, bringing major cost savings which in turn helped fend off competition from other modes of freight haulage. For example, BR had replaced two daily trains of aviation fuel from Lindsey to Langley with a single 3,000-tonne train. Smaller-scale flows operated from Lindsey and Humber to power stations in the Aire and Trent valleys, and in the reverse direction EWS moved trainloads of crude oil from Welton to Immingham.

While EWS kept most of its Immingham petroleum flows, there were some losses due to terminal closures such as those at Sunderland in 2001 and Leeds in 2002. The Heathrow Airport railhead at Langley also closed in 2003, but EWS continued to carry aviation fuel to the nearby Colnbrook terminal which had reopened in 1997. Bitumen traffic from Immingham gained a new lease of life when the Preston Docks branch reopened in 2004 with the support of a £2 million Freight Facilities Grant, providing a replacement terminal for Ashton-in-Makerfield. In 2001, Freightliner Heavy Haul started operating some petroleum trains from Immingham, but EWS kept the lion's share of the work and its position was strengthened in 2005, when it signed a five-year contract with Total to haul all rail-borne flows out of Lindsey. In 2006, EWS took delivery of 145 new tank wagons for the Total business, breaking the tradition of customer-owned petroleum wagons.

One small but relatively constant customer for petroleum trains was the Phillips plant at Port Clarence. EWS served a number of terminals from Port Clarence, including Glazebrook and Leeds in the early days and Westerleigh and Bedworth later on. Another source of petroleum traffic in the North East was Seal Sands, which sent fuel oil to several power stations in the early 2000s.

The BP refinery at Grangemouth had seen its rail output decline sharply in the early 1990s, leaving EWS with just one major flow to Dalston and smaller flows to Prestwick, Riccarton and Linkswood. A revival was heralded in 2000 when BP received a £10 million grant to install new rail loading facilities at Grangemouth and fund several new or refurbished receiving terminals. As a result, EWS successfully revived the flows from Grangemouth to Lairg and Fort William, but plans to introduce flows to Aberdeen, Kilmarnock and Maxwelltown never came to fruition.

Stanlow refinery had once been one of BR's biggest sources of petroleum traffic, but Shell had already switched many flows to pipeline or road transport by the time EWS was formed. In 1996, the main destination served by rail from Stanlow was Jarrow, once the subject of a high-profile contract renewal in Trainload Freight days. However, the Jarrow traffic was diverted

LEFT 37884 has just run round in Briton Ferry yard with 6V14, the 07.30 Saltend to Baglan Bay chemicals train, on 28 August 1998. The main flows to Baglan Bay at that time were acetic acid from Saltend and propylene from Humber.

BELOW A short section of the Swanage branch remained in revenue-earning freight use for liquefied petroleum gas from the Wytch Farm railhead at Furzebrook to Avonmouth. 66088 shunts TTA tanks in Furzebrook loop before departing with 6V29, the 20.29 train to Avonmouth, on 17 July 2000.

ABOVE One of the petroleum services from Fawley was a combined trainload of bitumen for Plymstock and gas oil for railway fuelling points in the South West. 66032 passes Dawlish Warren with 6V62, the 13.34 from Fawley to Tavistock Junction, on 18 July 2000.

RIGHT 56118 nears its destination with 6F60, the 07.25 from Warrington Arpley to Folly Lane, on 28 March 2002. Runcorn Folly Lane was one chemicals location that bucked the trend of cutbacks and closures, where INEOS Chlor built its new loading point for caustic soda.

to operate from Immingham at the start of 1998, after which the residual business still on rail at Stanlow was insufficient to keep the rail loading facility active. The last loaded tank train left Stanlow in March 1998.

In South Wales, EWS carried block trains of petroleum products from Robeston and Waterston refineries to distribution terminals at Westerleigh and Theale. Refining at Waterston ceased in 1997, but Robeston continued to provide some of EWS's heaviest trains, including 2,650-tonne loads bound for Westerleigh. Llandarcy refinery produced a small amount of outgoing fuel oil and bitumen traffic until 1999, after which it became the destination for block bitumen trains from Coryton. EWS also carried heavy fuel oil to several destinations from the Minimet oil storage terminal at Cardiff Docks, with the last regular service finishing in 2006.

The Esso refinery at Fawley was a longstanding user of pipelines and, by the 1990s, moved only around 5% of its output by rail. EWS carried a share of the traffic that was not suitable for pipelines, including gas oil to several railway fuelling points, liquefied petroleum gas (LPG) to Longport and bitumen to Plymouth Cattewater, also supplying Fawley with crude oil from Holybourne. The LPG and bitumen flows would end in 1997 and 2008 respectively. Another flow of LPG operated from the Wytch Farm oilfield railhead at Furzebrook to a distribution terminal at Avonmouth; this traffic ceased in 2005, when the output from Wytch Farm was no longer sufficient for a viable rail service.

On North Thameside, the Shell refinery at Shell Haven had stopped using rail in the early 1990s and closed altogether in 1999. The BP refinery at Coryton lost most of its rail traffic in BR days, but EWS was successful in starting up new flows from Coryton to Langley, Ipswich, Cambridge, Littlemore, Rugeley, Brownhills, Whittington, Lostock and Ferrybridge, adding up to around 10 trains a week. However, those trains had all ceased by 2003, leaving just a single flow of bitumen from Coryton to Llandarcy, which lingered until 2008. The Carless refinery at Harwich provided EWS with incoming trainloads of North Sea gas

RIGHT EWS ran 'jumbo' trains from the Immingham refineries to several receiving terminals, making good use of Class 60 traction. With 27 102-tonne tanks in tow, 60063 passes Stainforth with 6N02, the 09.00 Humber to Jarrow train, on 14 August 2001. The train will split into portions at Tyne Yard because of the restricted space at Jarrow.

condensate from North Walsham, plus outgoing flows of solvent to Longport and mud oil to Aberdeen (the latter product used as a lubricant on oil rigs). However, the Longport trains finished in 2001 and GB Railfreight took over the remaining Carless business in 2005.

Chemicals

Chemicals posed an even greater challenge than petroleum to EWS's marketing team. Many bulk chemical flows had disappeared in the 1980s and early 1990s, when changes to manufacturing systems reduced the need to transport large quantities of feedstock over large distances as the number of separate production sites diminished. Much of the chemicals traffic that remained on rail in 1996 was relatively low-volume, for which Enterprise or intermodal services offered the best solution.

Rail-borne carbon dioxide traffic was phased out, partly because of cheaper imports and partly because it was more cost-effective to manufacture close to point of use. The last carbon dioxide flow, which ran from Haverton Hill to Willesden, ceased in 1998. Another loss was the vinyl chloride monomer flow from Burn Naze to Barry, which finished in 1999 when the source was switched to a site without rail connection at Runcorn. Cutbacks by BP brought the closure of all rail operations at Saltend and reductions at Baglan Bay in early 2002. EWS lost its Humber to Stanlow and Baglan Bay propylene flows to Freightliner Heavy Haul in 2002, but both had ceased by 2004. The rail system at Haverton Hill, once a thriving centre for various flows of chemicals, handled its last revenue-earning freight traffic in 2002.

ABOVE EWS maintained a weekly train to Long Rock (Penzance) motive power depot for deliveries of gas oil from Fawley. 66160 waits to join the main line at Long Rock with 6C11, the 12.30 empties to St Blazey, on 18 April 2006.

On the positive side, EWS won a contract with Eastman Chemicals in early 1998 to move 4,000 containers a year of imported pure terephthalic acid from Teesport to Workington, initially for a three-year period. This contract required the provision of 20 refurbished intermodal wagons and loading gauge enhancements on the Cumbrian Coast line to accommodate 8ft 6in containers.

Chemicals traffic in Cheshire received a boost in 2001, when Albion Chemicals (formerly BP) gained a five-year contract to supply hydrochloric acid from its Sandbach plant to the DSM (formerly Roche Products) Vitamin C factory at Dalry. This traffic required the conversion of seven former petroleum tank wagons that were lined with rubber and equipped with automatic valves. The flow lasted until January 2007, when the rail connection at Sandbach was taken out of use.

Another success for EWS was the building of a new caustic soda loading terminal on the Runcorn Folly Lane branch for INEOS Chlor, supported by a £4 million Freight Facilities Grant. The terminal catered mainly for flows to Dalry and Mossend, with the first loaded train running in March 2002.

Rail-borne fertiliser traffic made a short-lived comeback in the late 1990s. Hydro Agri (formerly Norsk Hydro) reintroduced rail services from Immingham to destinations such as Avonmouth, Carmarthen and Carlisle. Kemira, which had phased out its rail-based distribution network from Ince & Elton in the early 1990s, made a tentative return to rail in 1999 when it used the AHC terminal at Widnes to load fertiliser for Lugton. Further Kemira traffic ran from Widnes and Warrington to Ely and Great Yarmouth. However, Kemira did not reopen its own rail connection at Ince & Elton and there was little prospect of regular high-volume traffic, as most of the company's regional distribution depots had been closed in favour of direct deliveries from the plant.

One new name in the rail-borne fertiliser business was J. & H. Bunn at Great Yarmouth. In 1998, EWS competed successfully for seasonal movements from Great Yarmouth to various railheads in southern England, using the Enterprise network as far as Wembley or Eastleigh and then dedicated feeder services as required. For a time these movements seemed to thrive. EWS even adapted a former Tiphook Piggyback wagon to carry a forklift truck, which travelled with each train for unloading. However, the J. & H. Bunn traffic ceased in 2000.

By the end of 2008, EWS carried just one trainload flow of chemicals in conventional wagons: styrene monomer from Immingham to Stalybridge.

ABOVE 66229 heads north on the York station avoiding line with 6E77, the 10.22 Westerleigh to Port Clarence empty tank train, on 31 May 2006. Petroleum tank wagons were traditionally painted in various shades of grey, but some owners adopted more colourful schemes such as green for BP and red for Murco and Petroplus.

LEFT Bitumen was conveyed to the Kelbit terminal at Ashton-in-Makerfield until the business moved to Preston Docks in 2004. 56090 backs down the Kelbit branch in order to join the West Coast main line with the empty tanks returning to Lindsey on 9 April 2003.

seven

Construction

For EWS's construction business, the fortunes of rail and road were inextricably linked. Roughly two thirds of rail-borne aggregates – stone, gravel and sand – were destined for new roads and motorways. This traffic had been one of BR's biggest growth areas in Trainload Freight days, but the recent scaling down of the government's road-building programme had put an end to that. From a peak of 17 million tonnes in 1988, rail-borne aggregates traffic had shrunk to 14 million in 1994 and just nine million tonnes in 1996.

LEFT 60021 *Star of the East* passes Ribblehead station with 16 FCA wagons forming 6E13, the 12.40 empties from Kirkby Thore to Drax, on 8 September 2004. It was gypsum from Drax to Kirkby Thore that brought regular revenue-earning freight back to the Settle & Carlisle line in BR days.

RIGHT The Parkandillack branch served clay dries at Blackpool, Kernick, Treviscoe and Parkandillack. Blackpool handled Fowey export traffic only, but the other dries served a range of destinations. 66116 shunts vans for mainland Europe and hoppers for Cliffe Vale at the south end of the Kernick/Treviscoe complex, on 25 February 2000.

By far the biggest destination region for aggregates was South East England, where locally sourced material was in short supply and the railway had gained a market share of approximately 80% on movements from quarries in the Mendips and Leicestershire. EWS remained the operator of the multi-portion 'jumbo' trains from Merehead and Whatley quarries to Acton yard, weighing up to 5,000 tonnes and hauled by Mendip Rail's Class 59 locomotives. Feeder services operated from Acton to more than a dozen terminals in the South East; EWS also ran direct trains from Merehead and Whatley to half a dozen locations in Hampshire, Berkshire and Oxfordshire.

Sea-dredged aggregates provided EWS with regular trainload business from Angerstein Wharf loading point on the Thames to a cluster of terminals in the London area, including Battersea, Paddington, Park Royal, King's Cross and Luton. Further aggregates flows within the South East operated from Cliffe to Purley and Salfords, from Newhaven to Crawley, and from Marks Tey to Hayes & Harlington. Rail could compete over short distances provided there was a sufficient volume of business.

In Leicestershire, EWS hauled trainloads of crushed granite from four quarries to a network of receiving terminals in East Anglia and the South East. The biggest single source was Mountsorrel, where roughly half the rail-borne output was carried in Redland's pioneering self-discharge trains. Smaller but still significant volumes of stone were transported from Croft, Bardon Hill and Cliffe Hill (Stud Farm) quarries.

Limestone from the Peak District accounted for roughly one quarter of EWS's total aggregates traffic. The railway served three quarries in the Buxton area: Buxton Lime Industries (formerly ICI) at Tunstead, RMC at Dove Holes, and Lafarge Redland at Dowlow. The biggest single flow from those quarries was 900,000 tonnes of limestone dispatched annually from Tunstead to the Brunner Mond chemical plants at Lostock and Oakleigh, both near Northwich. Until late 1997, this traffic used ageing ICI hopper wagons which, because they had vacuum brakes only, required Class 37 haulage instead of the Class 60s which worked most other stone trains in the area. Another exception was the limestone flow from Tunstead to the flue gas desulphurisation plant at Drax, operated by National Power with Class 59 haulage until EWS took over that company's rail operation in 1998.

In the Yorkshire Dales, EWS hauled trainloads of limestone from Rylstone quarry to distribution depots at Leeds and Hull. Further north EWS had no regular aggregates traffic, as the needs of the construction industry in

LEFT 37042 waits at Burngullow before continuing its journey from St Blazey to Parkandillack with empty CDA china clay hoppers, on 21 February 2000.

LEFT Uniquely Mendip Rail-liveried 59002 *Alan J Day* heads west near Longhedge Junction with 6V18, the 12.31 Hither Green to Whatley empties, on 3 April 2002. Hither Green was the gathering point for portions from Allington and Ardingly.

population centres such as Teesside and Glasgow were easily met by local sources where the use of rail would not be economic.

Cement traffic had declined sharply by the time EWS came into being, largely as a result of new distribution policies by the cement manufacturers. EWS carried bulk cement for Blue Circle from Hope (Earles Sidings) to Widnes, Northenden and Dewsbury, and from Oxwellmains to Viewpark, Aberdeen and Inverness, the last two flows making use of the Enterprise network. For Castle Cement, EWS ran a daily block train from Ketton to London King's Cross. Other building materials flows included the movement of Plasmor blocks from Heck to Biggleswade and Bow.

Household waste formed an important part of EWS's construction business, especially in the London area where trainloads of compacted and containerised waste operated from Brentford to Appleford, from Cricklewood to Stewartby, and from Northolt to Calvert. The former brick pits at Calvert were also the destination of a daily trainload of waste from three transfer stations in what had been (until 1996) the county of Avon: at Bath, Bristol and Westerleigh. In Greater Manchester, EWS operated waste trains from Northenden, Bredbury and Brindle Heath to a landfill site in former ironstone workings at Roxby, near Scunthorpe. Roxby also received trainloads of red gypsum waste from the Tioxide works at Grimsby. In Scotland, the company held a contract with Edinburgh City Council to haul household waste from Powderhall, on the former Granton branch; this traffic ran to Kaimes until 1997, when it switched to Oxwellmains.

EWS's industrial minerals traffic included china clay, gypsum, potash, rock salt and industrial sand. The china clay business was centred almost exclusively on Cornwall, where the company continued to provide an intensive service from several loading points to Fowey Docks using the CDA wagons which BR had introduced in the late 1980s. This traffic reached nearly 900,000 tonnes in 1998. EWS also moved china clay in block trains from Cornwall to Cliffe Vale for the Staffordshire pottery industry, and to Irvine for Caledonian Paper.

Gypsum traffic had returned to the railway in 1993, when the first desulphurisation plant came on stream at Drax power station. EWS took over BR's 10-year contract to move trainloads of gypsum from Drax to Kirkby Thore and Mountfield, extending the scope of the business by transporting imported gypsum

RIGHT EWS hauled trainloads of domestic refuse for the Greater Manchester Waste Disposal Authority until the contract passed to Freightliner Heavy Haul in 2008. 66122 is pictured at Dean Lane after working 6J44, the 15.28 feeder service from Pendleton, on 1 August 2001. The wagons had previously formed part of a Roxby to Pendleton train.

ABOVE A short-term flow of stone from Harrison's Sidings, Shap, to Ashton-in-Makerfield produced a weekly trainload of MEA wagons on the Cumbrian stretch of the West Coast main line. Both loaded and empty workings were staged at Carnforth for pathing and crewing purposes. 60096 passes Low Gill with train 6P50 from Carnforth to Harrison's Sidings on 6 August 2002.

from ports such as Workington, Hunterston and Southampton.

The Cleveland Potash mine at Boulby generated short-distance but high-volume traffic, with up to eight trains a day conveying potash and rock salt to Tees Dock and Middlesbrough. The British Industrial Sand quarry at Middleton Towers produced trainload flows to glassworks at Barnby Dun, Monk Bretton and Worksop.

With little prospect of a recovery in the construction industry in the short term, EWS needed to look for new openings if it was to increase its business overall. One such was fixed-term traffic for specific construction projects, for which the company was willing to provide temporary terminals and handling facilities. From 1997-9, EWS carried additional traffic from the Mendip quarries (*see right*).

In 1999, the previously mothballed Meldon branch was restored to use for short-term stone traffic from Flexer Construction to Crediton, Goodrington, Hackney (Newton Abbot), Taunton and Plymouth Friary – all new or revived locations for commercial railfreight.

In North West England, the building of the second runway at Manchester Airport brought substantial extra rail traffic from both Tunstead and Dove Holes, with a total of 1.4 million tonnes conveyed to a temporary terminal on the airport branch between December 1997 and late 1999. Meanwhile, tonnages from Rylstone were boosted in 1998 by the movement of some 100,000 tonnes of stone for the building of the A1/M1 link road near Leeds.

The building of the Channel Tunnel Rail Link (now known as High Speed One) generated a total of more than two million tonnes of aggregates traffic for EWS. Foster Yeoman supplied the bulk of the traffic, with two daily trains running from Merehead to Sevington. Additional volumes of sand and stone were moved from Grain to Sevington and from Whatley to Allington, the latter flow feeding the construction works for the North Downs tunnel.

Another area with good potential for growth was aggregates traffic from South Wales, where several quarries produced high-quality stone for use as a final dressing on road surfaces but lacked a rail connection. EWS offered to organise road transport for this traffic to nearby railheads and, by mid-1998, up to three or four trains a week were being moved from locations such as Steel Supply (Neath), Cwmbargoed and Cwmgwrach. The main destinations were Hayes, Ashford, Leeds Stourton and Leeds Hunslet (Cross Green). EWS also catered for flows of gritstone from Machen to Crawley in 1997 and from Newport Docks to Leeds in 1998.

One entirely new market was the movement of blast-furnace slag from steelworks for use in the construction industry – which had good potential in view of tax penalties that would soon be applied to traditionally quarried aggregates. Two contracts were signed between EWS and Cambrian Stone, the latter being a joint venture between British Steel and Tarmac. The first contract was for moving 40,000 tonnes of slag from Port Talbot to Godstone, for work at Gatwick Airport during 1998. The second was for one million tonnes from Llanwern to Cardiff

Additional traffic from the Mendip quarries, 1997-99

Receiving terminal	Project	Timescale
Minehead	Sea defences	March 1997-June 1998
Exeter	Honiton bypass	from February 1998
Avonmouth	Honda factory	September 1997-1998
Hamworthy	Puddletown bypass	July 1998-1999
Goodrington	Eurobell cable TV	from September 1998
Southampton Docks	Sea defences (Isle of Wight)	from September 1998

LEFT Despite some competition from Freightliner Heavy Haul, EWS held on to most of the limestone traffic out of the Peak District quarries, including the longstanding flow to Lostock and Oakleigh for Brunner Mond. 60078 approaches Great Rocks Junction with 25 empty JEA hoppers forming 6H03, the 08.47 from Oakleigh to Tunstead, on 10 April 2006.

Docks for use at Tremorfa water treatment works, starting in summer 1998.

As for EWS's long-standing aggregates flows, the tonnages railed from the Mendips started to recover and Mendip Rail abandoned its aspiration to open access. New destinations included a terminal at Exeter for Hanson, the owner of Whatley quarry. In 1999, EWS signed a new seven-year contract with Bardon Aggregates, soon to become part of Aggregate Industries, which included movements from Croft and South Wales as well as from Bardon Hill. In 2000, Aggregate Industries opened a new receiving depot on the former coal depot site at Neasden. The throughput at Neasden included a new flow of sand from Warmwell quarry, which was loaded on to rail at Wool.

In 2002, EWS won a seven-year contract with Lafarge to continue carrying granite from Mountsorrel to various depots across southern England. The self-discharge train allowed new destinations to be served with minimal investment in terminal facilities. One new location supplied from Mountsorrel in 2002 was Boston Docks, using the rail connection across the swing bridge which had been restored to use for steel traffic. In 2004, Lafarge established a new terminal at Small Heath, once again served by the self-discharge train.

The future of the Brunner Mond limestone traffic from Tunstead was assured when this company received a £6.1 million Freight Facilities Grant, the largest ever of its kind in England, to provide new rolling stock and discharge facilities at its Lostock and Oakleigh plants. The new stock entered service in 2000. Further growth in Peak District tonnages was achieved with the opening of new receiving terminals at Bredbury and Brierley Hill, and the re-fettling of an existing facility at Agecroft, as well as an increase in seasonal sugar stone deliveries to East Anglia. In 2003, EWS signed a seven-year contract with RMC to keep the Dove Holes traffic on rail. In the same year, EWS started carrying tankloads of powdered lime mortar from Dove Holes to Bletchley, initially attached to the bulk limestone train but later conveyed by the wagonload network.

In the cement market EWS lost out to competition from Freightliner Heavy Haul, which took over the Blue Circle flows from Hope to Dewsbury and the new Weaste terminal in 2000. FHH would eventually take over all Blue Circle (later Lafarge) cement flows from Hope and Oxwellmains. On the credit side, EWS renewed its agreement with Castle Cement for traffic from Ketton in 2002 and won a major contract to convey cement from the new Buxton Lime Industries plant at Tunstead to distribution terminals at Leeds, Walsall and Willesden, starting in 2004.

Hopes of an expansion of waste traffic were dampened by the trend away from landfill in favour of incineration and recycling. Existing flows of household waste faced competition from FHH, which took over the Bristol/Bath traffic in 2001 and later the flows from Cricklewood and the Greater Manchester railheads. EWS was the transport partner in an

RIGHT 60055 *Thomas Barnardo*, still in Trainload Freight livery with Transrail markings, approaches Aylesbury station with 6E34, the 13.54 Calvert to King's Cross empty spoil train, on 19 August 2004. The inward working carried spoil from the building site that would become the Channel Tunnel Rail Link.

ABOVE 66121 draws forward at Penmaenmawr during the loading of 6Z52, the 10.47 departure for Acton, on 17 April 2004. The stone in this instance was destined for the White City redevelopment. The main flow from Penmaenmawr quarry was railway ballast, but customers in the general construction industry were served as well.

ambitious scheme to convey residual waste from an industrial recycling plant at Bow to Calvert in 2001, but this traffic never amounted to more than a few trial trains. The flow of red gypsum waste from Grimsby to Roxby ceased in 2001.

The building of Terminal 5 at Heathrow Airport generated large volumes of railfreight to a temporary terminal at Colnbrook, on the former Staines West branch. While Freightliner Heavy Haul delivered the cement, EWS was contracted to move regular trainloads of stone from the Mendips, as well as pulverised fly ash from West Burton power station. The fly ash (also known as PFA) was carried in 'tanktainers' painted in Rugby Cement's bright orange livery. The use of fly ash as a low-grade construction material had been identified as a growth area by EWS due to the tax now levied on primary aggregates.

The largely self-contained china clay operation in Cornwall stayed with EWS, thanks to the renewal of a five-year contract with Imerys in late 2004. However, the Cornish product faced ever stiffer competition from cheaper foreign supplies and the long-distance traffic from Cornwall to the Potteries and Scotland declined. The block train flow of clay slurry from Burngullow to Irvine, once hailed as the longest-distance block train in the UK, gave way in December 2007 to a service conveying Brazilian clay from Antwerp. The tonnages of Cornish product shipped through Fowey declined as both Imerys and EWS rationalised their operations, with longer trains running from fewer terminals.

In early 2005, EWS fended off competition from other operators and signed a 10-year contract with Mendip Rail, with provision for new flows and increased tonnages in line with market needs. On the debit side, the company lost a number of aggregates flows to Freightliner Heavy Haul during 2005, including Dowlow to Kennett and Barham, Bardon Hill to Thorney Mill, and Tunstead to Ratcliffe. A new flow from Mountsorrel to Luton also went to FHH, although EWS held the long-term traffic for existing Mountsorrel traffic. More business switched from EWS to FHH in 2006, including Wool to Neasden, Croft to Bow and Neasden, and various flows from Bardon Hill and Jersey Marine.

EWS gained a substantial fixed-term freight flow following a decision by Vale Royal Borough Council to fill long-abandoned salt mines under the town of Northwich, to protect buildings from subsidence and allow future development. From January 2005 until August 2007, trainloads of fly ash from Drax were delivered to a temporary terminal beside the Brunner Mond works at Oakleigh, using two 16-vehicle rakes of EWS's MBA bogie box wagons. EWS also expected to carry brine from Oakleigh and converted a small fleet of tank wagons for that purpose; however, in the event, the brine was not transported by rail.

The years 2007-08 brought mixed fortunes for EWS, as major contracts came up for renewal. Freightliner Heavy Haul took over the Cleveland potash traffic from Boulby in 2007, which – when combined with falling volumes of steel traffic – weakened EWS's position on Teesside considerably. The Greater Manchester waste traffic switched to FHH in 2008, the contract extended to a 25-year term in 2009. On the other hand, EWS won back several flows previously operated by FHH or GB Railfreight, including Stud Farm to Bury St Edmunds, and Dove Holes to Hitchin.

A piece of good news in the once depressed cement market was the revival of traffic from Clitheroe in 2008. EWS won the contract to move trainloads of cement from Clitheroe to Mossend, bringing additional freight to the Settle & Carlisle line and recalling the days of the Clitheroe to Gunnie trains which had ceased in the early 1990s.

ABOVE Once sold by National Power to EWS, the Class 59/2s were used on various flows but settled down on aggregates trains in the South of England, working alongside the Mendip Rail '59/0s' and '59/1s'. 59205 passes Wanstrow on the Merehead branch with 7C77, the 12.40 empties from Acton to Merehead, on 4 April 2007. The train includes JNA wagons from Harlow and Woking, and KEA wagons from Battersea.

RIGHT 60031 approaches Normanton station with 6M22, the 11.20 Leeds to Tunstead cement empties, on 17 July 2006. The contract to move cement from the new Buxton Lime Industries plant at Tunstead compensated EWS for the loss of the Lafarge cement business.

LEFT 66141 passes Saxilby with FCA intermodal wagons forming 6V25, the 13.40 departure from West Burton, on 21 July 2006. From 2003 until 2006, EWS moved containerised fly ash from West Burton to Colnbrook, the railhead for Heathrow Airport construction work. Fly ash is a low-value commodity that tends to be used for specific projects requiring fixed-term transport contracts.

RIGHT The Corus plant at Redcar received a thrice-weekly train of limestone dust from Harrison's Sidings, near Hardendale, using hooded HFA hopper wagons. 60045 *The Permanent Way Institution* passes Grangetown with the final stage of this working, 6N25 from Tees Yard to Redcar, on 1 June 2007.

LEFT 60059 *Swinden Dalesman* provides appropriate traction for 6D71, the 16.16 Rylstone to Healey Mills train, as it comes off the branch at Skipton on 13 July 2008. EWS retained the long-term traffic flows from Rylstone (Swinden) quarry against competition from other operators.

ABOVE The Guardian glassworks at Goole was a new destination for sand from Middleton Towers. 66180 edges forward at Goole while its train of PAA hoppers is loaded on 24 May 2007. It will later depart as 6H93, the 17.04 from Goole to Peterborough.

eight

Enterprise and Intermodal

Even in Transrail days, the Enterprise network had made incursions into areas that were mainly Loadhaul or Mainline Freight territory. For example, Transrail hauled calcium carbonate from Quidhampton to Sittingbourne via its Willesden hub, a journey made entirely via Mainline Freight routes. Transrail identified serious potential for wagonload traffic to and from the North East ports, very much the heartland of Loadhaul, while in the South East it planned to dovetail with RfD's Connectrail service for train ferry and Channel Tunnel flows. Cooperation between Transrail and RfD had already been happening on a limited scale, such as the Enterprise service to Aberdeen which conveyed Connectrail as well as Enterprise traffic.

LEFT 47760 *Ribblehead Viaduct* rounds the curve from Wakefield Kirkgate to Calder Bridge Junction with train 6D36, the 11.04 from Doncaster to Wakefield, on 12 April 1999. The load on this occasion comprises one JSA wagon with coil from Port Talbot and two IGA flat wagons with steel tubing from Germany. The Cobra distribution terminal at Wakefield thrived as the Enterprise network expanded. It handled flows of paper and bottled water alongside its core business of steel products.

RIGHT East Anglian wagonload flows, including traffic to and from the Potter Group at Ely, were variously routed via Doncaster or London. On 29 May 1998, RES locomotive 47789 *Lindisfarne* approaches its destination with 6E77, the 13.05 from Ely to Doncaster Belmont – a long journey for just one wagon!

Under EWS management, the boundaries between Transrail, Loadhaul and Mainline Freight territories were quickly forgotten. In January 1997, EWS introduced a new train plan for North East England, with a single out-and-back train between Lackenby and Warrington calling at Tees Yard, Healey Mills and Blackburn on the outward run, and additionally at Wakefield on the return. This service made efficiency savings as it replaced three separate trains: the thrice-weekly Enterprise service between Warrington and Tees Yard, a similarly regular block steel train between Lackenby and Blackburn, and an Enterprise feeder service between Warrington and Blackburn. The revised train carried new flows of steel coil from Port Talbot and Llanwern to Wakefield, alongside existing traffic such as steel coil from Lackenby to Blackburn, steel rods from Sheerness to Blackburn, and caustic soda from Port Clarence to Dalry.

EWS opened up South Humberside to Enterprise traffic by diverting the daily train between Immingham and Wolverhampton Steel Terminal to run via the West Midlands Enterprise hub at Bescot, instead of via Washwood Heath. This change enabled EWS to carry wagonloads of imported zinc ingots from Grimsby to Bloxwich.

In South East England, EWS consolidated Transrail's gain of finished steel products out of Sheerness. The Sheerness to Willesden feeder service was increased to run on five instead of three days a week, and to convey wagonloads of pulp from Sheerness Docks to Workington for Iggesund Paperboard – as well as steel and other traffic to and from the recently established Victa Railfreight terminal at Sittingbourne.

South West England benefited from a new daily Enterprise working in January 1997 between Newport Alexandra Dock Junction (ADJ) and St Blazey, calling at Hallen Marsh (Avonmouth), Exeter and Tavistock Junction. The principal traffic on this train was coal from South Wales to Tavistock Junction for Plymstock cement works,

LEFT 37427, one of the first Class 37s to carry EWS livery, passes Greenhill Lower Junction with 6D35, the 11.40 Grangemouth to Mossend Enterprise train, on 16 July 1998. This service could carry intermodal and conventional wagonload traffic as required.

LEFT 37225 passes Northam steel terminal on 20 July 1998 with 6Y26, the 08.28 Eastleigh to Quidhampton Enterprise train, conveying five bogie tanks which would be reloaded with calcium carbonate for Workington, Mossend or Corpach.

but it also catered for other flows such as lead shot from Falmouth, calcified seaweed from Truro and electrical goods from Bodmin. The Avonmouth area offered much potential, with flows of paper, bottled water and cars lending themselves to wagonload movement.

The timetable change of June 1997 brought a further shake-up of the Enterprise network, partly as a result of continued traffic growth and partly because EWS was in the process of acquiring RfD. The company wanted to reap the benefits of integrating Enterprise and Connectrail as quickly as possible. The West Coast main line was the busiest route for Enterprise, and EWS expanded the service on that corridor to three trains daily in each direction between Wembley and Warrington, five between Warrington and Carlisle, and four between Carlisle and Mossend.

The flagship West Coast train became a 75mph service, running nightly in both directions between Wembley and Mossend and making intermediate calls at Daventry and Warrington Arpley. The scheduled transit time between Wembley and Mossend of just over eight hours made rail a viable proposition for time-sensitive traffics, previously hauled by road. One flow that made good use of the fast service was paper from Aberdeen to Northampton, in prototype Roadrailer bi-modal vehicles. The 75mph train also carried wagonloads of paper from Aberdeen to France and bottled water from Inverness to several distribution depots. Unlike other Enterprise trains on the West Coast main line, the 75mph service was electrically hauled throughout – using a Class 90 locomotive hired from RfD, pending the sale of RfD to EWS.

A further example of shared operation between EWS and RfD was the revised nightly service between Carlisle and Eastleigh. Previously, this route had been covered by RfD services between Carlisle and Crewe and then Crewe and Eastleigh, sponsored by the Ministry of Defence. From June 1997 the service called at Bescot instead of Crewe, becoming available to EWS as well as RfD traffic. The EWS business included pulp from Sheerness to Workington on the Bescot to Carlisle leg, and calcium carbonate from Quidhampton to Scotland on the Eastleigh to Bescot leg.

The Eastleigh link created further business opportunities for EWS in the Hampshire area, with an intermediate call at Didcot catering for traffic to and from Didcot Milton distribution centre which had seen little rail traffic since the 1980s. The Didcot call also allowed the

RIGHT The two prototype Eurospine wagons seemed to perform well on their daily run carrying specially adapted Parcelforce trailers between Willesden and Mossend, but the experiment failed to generate long-term business. The trailers are pictured awaiting unloading at Mossend on 15 July 1998.

RIGHT Ministry of Defence business featured strongly in the wagonload throughput at Eastleigh yard, with trips operating to Marchwood military port and Ludgershall. 47314 *Transmark* passes Millbrook with train 6B46, the 09.02 from Marchwood to Eastleigh, on 20 July 1998.

interchange of wagons with the nightly RfD service between Newport ADJ and Wembley.

EWS made several changes to Enterprise operations in the London area in June 1997. It transferred most Enterprise marshalling from Willesden Brent yard to the RfD-owned Wembley European Freight Operations Centre, enabling an easier interface between Enterprise and Connectrail services. However, the overnight Bescot to Sittingbourne Enterprise service continued to call at Willesden Brent, to detach wagonloads of carbon dioxide for the adjacent Distillers terminal.

Additional trip workings around London for Enterprise flows included services from Wembley to Gidea Park, Purfleet and Tilbury. The Gidea Park terminal had been a casualty of RfD cutbacks in 1996, but was now once again able to handle Connectrail traffic in addition to new Enterprise flows. Purfleet dispatched regular container loads of aviation fuel to Georgemas Junction for Wick Airport, while the Tilbury train conveyed mainly imported chemical pulp destined for Workington.

The Enterprise service to North Kent increased to become twice daily in June 1997. One train served Hoo Junction, while others catered mainly for traffic to and from Sittingbourne, Queenborough and Sheerness. In order to avoid unnecessary marshalling, and because most wagons from North Kent were destined for the Midlands and North, the departing service from Sheerness ran through to Bescot without calling at Willesden or Wembley en route.

In South Wales and the South West, two major changes took place in June 1997. Firstly, EWS catered for heavy loads to northern England by running a second daily service between Avonmouth, Newport ADJ and Warrington. The additional train connected at Warrington with the 75mph West Coast main line Enterprise service and enabled the overnight transit of time-sensitive products between Avonmouth and central Scotland.

Secondly, EWS replaced the former Connectrail service which followed a triangular Wembley-Washwood Heath-ADJ-Wembley route with a two-way service between Wembley and ADJ. This reduced wasteful mileage and marshalling in the West Midlands for traffic from London to South Wales, while the change of traction from an RfD Class 47 to an EWS Class 56 usefully increased capacity as the eastbound service, in particular, was often heavily loaded. From ADJ, EWS provided an Enterprise trip working to the newly opened timber siding at Pontrilas, using a RES Class 47 locomotive in marginal time.

In North West England, EWS diverted the Sandbach trip working to call at Crewe for Connectrail traffic to the Steventon distribution depot. The trip to Dee Marsh Junction was rescheduled as a through train from Mossend to cater for increased volumes of timber to

LEFT EWS built on the Transrail presence in North Kent and served a number of customers by means of trip workings from Hoo Junction yard. Still carrying its former BR 'Civilink' livery, 31203 sets out from Hoo Junction with 6U74, the 09.46 departure to Sittingbourne, conveying china clay slurry from Burngullow on 19 July 1999.

LEFT Packages of pulp for Barrow-in-Furness are loaded into GE Capital vans at Sheerness Docks on 19 July 1999. For a time EWS had success with various flows of timber, paper and pulp.

Shotton Paper. The reopened Kronospan siding at Chirk gained a more frequent service, both for inward timber and for outward trial movements of finished product.

The North West gained two further Enterprise services in August 1997. One was a northbound extension of the Harwich to Doncaster train, providing a link for wagonload traffic between East Anglia and the North West and Scotland. The other was a new Enterprise train linking Warrington, Wakefield, Healey Mills and Immingham, catering mainly for containers and palletised paper to and from the port of Immingham.

EWS introduced its first East Coast main line Enterprise service in June 1997, linking Tees Yard, Millerhill, Thornton, Montrose and Aberdeen. The initial flows on this train were agricultural lime from Thrislington to Montrose and cement from Oxwellmains to Aberdeen. In August the train was extended southwards to run to and from Wakefield, mainly to cater for a new flow of Superdrug products from Wakefield to the TDG Harris warehouse at Mossend. This flow was established just three weeks after the initial enquiry from the customer – a good example of the flexibility that Enterprise provided. The East Coast train also carried containers from Tees Dock to Mossend for P&O and North Sea Ferries.

Timber traffic from Scotland and the border counties continued to grow. Among the new loading points established in 1997 were Laurencekirk, Dunkeld, Beattock, Carlisle Upperby and Hexham. The siding at Hexham also received wagonloads of timber for the nearby Egger factory. In the North of Scotland, the increase in timber and other wagonload traffic led EWS to introduce a second daily Enterprise train between Aberdeen and Elgin and a second daily train between Mossend and Fort William. Special trains carried spot loads of timber from Kyle of Lochalsh and Dunrobin.

The years 1998-99 saw further growth for Enterprise. In May 1998, Doncaster Belmont yard was re-fettled to supersede Healey Mills as the hub for Yorkshire and the East Coast ports. Its location on the East Coast main line gave it a strategic advantage compared with Healey Mills, served by trunk trains to Harwich, Wembley, Bescot, Warrington, Tees and Aberdeen, with feeder services running to Selby, Hull, Immingham, Wakefield, Aldwarke and Ely. From 1999, Doncaster was served by a new trunk service linking Corby with Mossend via the Settle to Carlisle line, and by a diverted metals train between Lackenby and Margam.

This expansion of the network was fuelled by numerous new wagonload flows. For a time, Enterprise looked like becoming a reincarnation of Speedlink. Grain traffic returned, with a 12-week contract from Andover to Roseisle using six IRB wagons imported from France. Animal feeds were carried from Ely to Scotland and, on a trial basis, from New Holland to Selby. EWS even carried a few vanloads of seed potatoes on routes such as Inverness to Thornaby, Inverness to Selby, Inverness to Ely, Elgin to Rugby, and Aberdeen to St Blazey – the first time potatoes had moved by rail since the 1980s.

In the paper sector, EWS gained a regular flow of pulp from Sheerness to Barrow-in-Furness for Kimberly-Clark and short-term pulp movements from Aberdeen, Montrose, Dundee and Grangemouth to Corpach for Arjo Wiggins.

RIGHT Victa Railfreight staff unload paper from Irvine out of an IZA van at Tilbury Grain Terminal on 29 July 1999. EWS developed a number of freight flows in partnership with Victa Railfreight, who took responsibility for terminal operations.

RIGHT The signalbox and semaphores lend a period feel to this view of 66093 passing Rainford with train 6E30, the 10.55 from Knowsley to Immingham, on 27 July 2001. The containers and vans had all carried imported paper and were returning to Immingham for reloading.

Some of the wagons that carried pulp from Tilbury to Workington for Iggesund were backloaded with finished product for export. Stora Enso also used Enterprise to carry imported newsprint from Immingham to Glasgow Deanside, in addition to its established trainload service to Barking. Import flows via the Channel Tunnel included paper reels from Germany and Austria to various terminals (including Stratford and Ely) and chipboard from Austria to Selby, from where it was delivered by road to Hygena at Howden and Egger at Hexham.

International Paper forwarded their home-produced product in vans from Aberdeen to France via the Channel Tunnel, and in containers to Belgium via Purfleet. There was also domestic container traffic from Aberdeen to Ely and Daventry. Arjo Wiggins at Corpach produced a regular flow of finished product to Cardiff and occasional wagonloads to Avonmouth and Purfleet. Caledonian Paper at Irvine dispatched paper to Antwerp via the Channel Tunnel and to Purfleet for local distribution. EWS also won a substantial two-way flow between Irvine and Shotton, with magazine paper moving south for the English and Welsh market and newsprint going back north for the Scottish market.

Raw timber continued to thrive. EWS reached an estimated market share of 80-90% of long-distance flows from loading points north of the Central Belt, reducing to 40% from the Scottish Borders. Alongside the established traffic to Shotton, Chirk and Pontrilas, EWS moved logs to Boat of Garten, Carlisle, Hereford and Cardiff for BSW, to Elgin for James Jones, and to Nairn for Gordon's. In 1998-99, more than 20 timber loading points were in use and the volume of traffic required not only EWS's 250 OTA stanchioned timber wagons but also

Timber loading points, 1998-99

Thurso
Kyle of Lochalsh
Inverness
Elgin
Huntly
Inverurie
Laurencekirk
Dunkeld
Stirling
Fort William
Oban
Taynuilt
Crianlarich
Arrochar
Deanside
Irvine
Beattock
Carlisle Upperby
Hexham
Tees Yard
Brandon
Eastleigh
Exeter Riverside

LEFT Kronospan invested in rail facilities at its Chirk factory in the 1980s, but it was not until the late 1990s that incoming timber traffic started to grow. Logs from Arrochar and Beattock are unloaded from OTA wagons at Chirk on 6 August 1999.

LEFT 60045 *The Permanent Way Institution* passes Stainforth with 6D65, the 10.07 Doncaster Belmont to Immingham Enterprise service, on 25 August 2000. The load includes a typical mixture of steel coil, paper and chemicals traffic.

its OBA open wagons, bogie IGA and IOB flat wagons hired from GE Rail Services.

The Ministry of Defence increased its use of rail, especially after the formation of the Defence Logistics Organisation which combined the logistics wings of the three armed forces. The MoD signed a new five-year contract with EWS in 1999 to cover a daily wagonload service on the core network and special trainload movements as required. The MoD's Longtown depot benefited from a new £5.5 million road-rail transfer facility, while the Redmire branch was reopened for trainloads of military vehicles for Catterick garrison, and the Mid-Norfolk Railway line to East Dereham carried traffic to the nearby Robertson barracks. The rail connection to Ashchurch was reactivated and special trains reached off-the-beaten-track locations including Pembroke Dock, Caerwent, Wool and Shoeburyness.

Wagonload traffic via the Channel Tunnel benefited from the full integration of Enterprise and Connectrail services. In December 1998, EWS introduced a direct wagonload service between Wembley and Cologne-Gremberg yard, cutting out the need for time-consuming marshalling in France and giving greatly improved journey times to and from Germany. The Europe-bound train was heavily loaded with steel from Port Talbot, Llanwern and Rotherham, while the return service carried flows such as chemicals from Ludwigshafen to Immingham, coiled steel rod from Duisburg to Longport, chipboard from Brilon to Selby, and aluminium from Singen to Wolverhampton.

Even more promisingly, EWS was claiming a toehold in the highly prized, fast-moving consumer goods market, especially the food and drink sector. With 300 million tonnes of food and drink consumed in Britain each year, even a small increase in the railway's market share would be significant. EWS used conventional vans to convey palletised goods for Superdrug from Wakefield to Mossend and from Mossend to Hoo Junction, for Sainsbury's between Mossend and Dagenham, and for Safeway between Hoo Junction, Daventry, Wakefield and Mossend.

Intermodal traffic was increasingly valued. EWS had entered the market by using its Enterprise network to carry containers in less-than-trainload quantities, reaching locations such as Teesport, Hull and Immingham which were not served by Freightliner. Teesport was especially fruitful. EWS also introduced new trunk intermodal trains from Harwich to Newport, Widnes and Seaforth, plus feeder services from Warrington Arpley to Widnes and Seaforth. New intermodal railheads were established at Plymouth Friary and Swansea Docks, while the Dow Corning terminal at Barry started to produce intermodal as well as conventional wagon traffic.

To cater for its intermodal services, EWS began using a mixture of 'Multifret' (FIA/IFA), Tiphook (KFA) and ex-Freightliner (FFA/FGA) wagons, all of which could carry containers up

RIGHT 66087 leaves Didcot with train 4B24, the 15.33 to Cardiff Pengam, on 16 August 2000. This traffic flow was later diverted to Wentloog, while the small yard at Didcot was also the base for Ministry of Defence feeder services to Bicester and Kineton, as well as Cardiff Pengam.

ABOVE The return of freight to the Far North line was strengthened by the Safeway intermodal traffic to Georgemas Junction. 66109 passes Rogart with the northbound train from Inverness to Georgemas Junction on 23 August 2001.
GAVIN MORRISON

to 8ft 6in high on most routes. As part of the Thrall Car building programme, it introduced three further wagon types: 400 FCA wagons with a deck height of 1023mm, 300 FKA wagons with a deck height of 820mm, and 100 FAA well wagons with a deck height of 712mm. The FKA and FAA types enabled the company to cater for the rising number of 9ft and 9ft 6in boxes on the network.

In March 1999, EWS launched its high-profile intermodal service for high-street retailer Safeway, carrying foodstuffs in refrigerated swap bodies from Mossend to Inverness. The train was later extended to Georgemas Junction, supplying Safeway stores in Caithness and the Orkney Islands. EWS was also keen to embrace bimodal technology: in 1998 the company took delivery of two prototype sets of KDA Eurospine wagons, built by Thrall Car, which it used to carry Parcelforce trailers between Willesden Euroterminal and Mossend.

After the departure of Ed Burkhardt in 1999, the expansion of Enterprise slowed. Doubts were expressed once again about the viability of wagonload in a small country such as Britain. Some economies were made to bring costs more closely in line with revenue, such as the thinning out of Enterprise trains in northern Scotland and South West England. Nevertheless, most individual flows kept going.

Meanwhile, the intermodal market was buoyant. In autumn 1999, EWS made its first direct challenge to Freightliner in carrying deep-sea containers from Felixstowe – loaded on to rail at Ipswich – and Southampton.

In 2000, new Enterprise flows included tissue products from Germany to the reopened distribution terminal at Ordsall Lane, timber from Law Junction to Chirk, and military vehicles to and from Ashchurch. On the debit side, Cerestar starch traffic from Trafford Park ceased, as did Croxton & Garry traffic from Melton. The first half of 2001 produced a similar pattern of gains and losses, with new flows of paper from Irvine to Daventry and from Immingham to Knowsley balancing traffic losses such as the pulp traffic from Sheerness to Barrow-in-Furness.

From mid-2001 onwards, the tide turned and Enterprise traffic began to ebb away. One of the first casualties was the Fitzgerald Lighting traffic from Bodmin, which used a short stretch of the Bodmin & Wenford Railway to join the national network at Bodmin Parkway. The customer in this instance faced a 100% price increase if he wished to stay on rail. Other losses included pulp to Workington and Corpach, bottled water from Inverness, Spillers pet food between Deanside and Wisbech, and all raw timber flows – except traffic from the West Highland line and Carlisle to Chirk, and occasional trainloads from the lineside loading point at Kinbrace to Inverness. One boost for the Far North line in 2002 was the opening of a grant-aided terminal at Thurso to receive building supplies from Law Junction and Inverness, but this traffic failed to reach viable volumes and would last only until 2004.

Wagonload traffic via the Channel Tunnel suffered severely after an influx of asylum seekers led to the near-total stoppage of Channel Tunnel freight in November 2001. A number of flows were permanently lost and several distribution railheads closed, including

LEFT 66042 passes Ripple Lane with a mixture of FKA, FIA and FCA wagons forming train 6M65, the 14.05 from Purfleet to Wembley, on 24 August 2001. The traffic on this occasion was destined for Seaforth and Barry. While Freightliner struggled to fill a regular intermodal train from Purfleet, EWS was able to provide a service from the port thanks to its Enterprise network.

RIGHT 92027 passes Rowell with train 6X12, the 17.15 from Carlisle to Eastleigh, conveying empty tanks from Workington, long-welded rail from Workington, and MoD traffic in vans and containers on 6 June 2007. If all wagonload trains had been as well loaded as this one, then the Enterprise network might well have survived.

Creative Logistics at Ordsall Lane, DCA Link at Cardiff Canton, and EWS at Longport.

But not all the news was bad. One Enterprise customer that bucked the trend was Stora Enso, which used a combination of trainload and Enterprise services to move imported paper from Immingham, Felixstowe and Zeebrugge to distribution terminals at Barking, Selby, Knowsley, Avonmouth and Deanside. EWS used the Stora Enso business as the basis of a daily feeder service to Knowsley that could also carry other wagonload traffic.

On the intermodal side, EWS concentrated increasingly on developing trainload flows, mostly targeting deep-sea containers. In 2003, it launched Intermodal Express, which covered trains from Felixstowe to Widnes and Wakefield, Southampton to Hams Hall, Widnes and Wakefield, Thamesport to Widnes, and Hams Hall to Glasgow Deanside. Further gains included traffic for Argos and IKEA on routes such as Southampton to Burton-on-Trent and Felixstowe to Ely. However, some planned additions to the network did not materialise – such as Stranraer, where gradients on the line of route made it impossible to carry viable volumes.

Some intermodal innovations were unsuccessful. Plans to run regular 90mph intermodal trains between London and Glasgow were shelved after apparently successful trials for P&O Nedlloyd, as the benefits of a shorter journey time were outweighed by the reduced axle loading – and therefore lower payload – incurred by the higher speed. The bimodal Parcelforce traffic to Mossend was withdrawn in 2002 and the plan to build 20 more Eurospine sets quietly forgotten.

In 2004-05, EWS tightened its policy on wagonload intermodal traffic and withdrew most flows that carried less than a full trainload. It also lost the Safeway traffic to Inverness after the supermarket chain sold its Highlands stores to Somerfield, whose distribution centre at Dundee was unsuited to rail movement from Mossend. On the positive side, EWS began a new trainload service between Hams Hall and Tilbury, designed for 9ft 6in containers and connecting with sailings to and from Rotterdam and Bilbao. Later that year the company started a short-distance Thamesport to Willesden service for Containerlift, but the economics of that operation were poor and it lasted only a few months.

As for conventional wagon traffic, EWS continued to shift business between trainload and Enterprise where it made economic sense to do so. In September 2004, it replaced the St Blazey to Cliffe Vale clay train – and occasional block loads of scrap metal from Plymouth to Cardiff – with a single train from Tavistock Junction to Cardiff Tidal, conveying clay, scrap metal and any other available freight. The

RIGHT The compact freight yard at Warrington Dallam was used for various flows of steel, containers and chemicals. 56110 waits at Dallam while its train is reloaded on 1 August 2001. It will depart as 4Z59, the 11.29 to Glasgow Deanside.

weekly trainload of china clay from Cornwall to Sezzadio became an Enterprise movement in 2005, with the loaded wagons routed via Eastleigh and Wembley and the return empties routed via Wembley and Cardiff.

EWS combined flows of export steel from Lackenby and Scunthorpe to Mostyn and paper from Immingham to Knowsley on the trans-Pennine route in order to cut out wasteful duplication of resources. Fuel oil from Grangemouth to Sinfin became an Enterprise movement as far as Doncaster, with a weekly feeder service operating from Doncaster to Sinfin. EWS continued to move occasional loads of contaminated drill cuttings from Aberdeen and Hamworthy to Lowestoft, using Enterprise services to Wembley and special trains as required from Wembley to Lowestoft.

Stora Enso changed its distribution arrangements in 2005, withdrawing from Felixstowe and setting up a new import terminal at Tilbury. Much of the former Felixstowe traffic now travelled by rail from Tilbury instead, but the Channel Tunnel flow from Zeebrugge to Barking ceased. Elsewhere in the paper industry, UPM-Kymmene continued to despatch by rail from Irvine to Daventry but ended the two-way traffic between Irvine and Shotton.

Some Enterprise traffic was lost not through any fault of EWS, but because of changes in the industries it serves – illustrating how the railway had to find new business just to stand still in terms of overall tonnage. The long-established flow of imported white goods to Paddock Wood ended abruptly in 2005 following a warehouse fire, while the last remaining freight flow to Corpach – calcium carbonate from Quidhampton – ceased when the Arjo Wiggins plant closed in September 2005. On the positive side, rail traffic from the Anglesey Aluminium plant at Holyhead resumed with a weekly consignment of billet to Austria, which would last until the plant closed in 2009.

The year 2006 brought further pruning of the Enterprise network. Several lightly loaded trip workings were withdrawn, such as those to Ridham Dock, Birmingham Lawley Street and Selby. The last EWS-operated timber flow, which served Kronospan at Chirk, was handed over to Amec-Spie at the end of the year.

RIGHT Although Wakefield Europort never came close to fulfilling its potential as a Channel Tunnel railhead, it gave EWS a convenient base for offloading maritime containers from Southampton, Felixstowe and Tilbury. 66152 and 66077 stand at Wakefield Europort on 18 February 2004, having worked 6E45 from Felixstowe and 6E98 from Wembley respectively.

LEFT Grangemouth saw a railfreight revival with new terminals operated by Malcolm, TDG and Forth Ports. 66096 waits at the TDG terminal before departing with train 6M67, the 18.01 from Grangemouth to Trafford Park, on 27 August 2003. Unfortunately, neither Grangemouth nor Trafford Park could sustain a viable throughput and both terminals were mothballed under DB Schenker management.

Intermodal changes included the withdrawal of trains from Felixstowe and Southampton to Ely, as the distance covered by rail was too short. EWS also withdrew one of its two daily trains on the Daventry to Mossend route after the haulage firm Russells switched its business to Direct Rail Services.

In 2007, the longstanding flow of French bottled water to Neasden was diverted to the recently built Prologis Park terminal at Coventry. Another diversion saw Stora Enso replace Knowsley with Stanton Grove (Liverpool Docks) as its Merseyside railhead, a change which led to the end of rail traffic to the Potter Group terminal at Knowsley. Towards the end of the year, EWS also lost the substantial wagonload flow of automotive parts from Germany to Birch Coppice.

High hopes for Scottish intermodal traffic were raised in 2008 as a £4 million gauge enhancement scheme was completed, allowing 8ft 6in containers to be carried on standard wagons to Aberdeen and Elgin. EWS introduced a weekly service between Grangemouth and Elgin, although it was routed via the Highland main line instead of Aberdeen to share haulage with the oil tanks to Lairg. The service was soon withdrawn due to poor loadings.

Wagonload changes in 2008 included the withdrawal of metals trip workings to Mostyn, Bristol East and Burton-on-Trent and the closure of Bescot and Doncaster Belmont yards as marshalling locations. EWS withdrew its direct train from Wembley to Avonmouth following the loss of Stora Enso traffic, replacing it with a weekly feeder service from Newport ADJ which carried chipboard from Switzerland.

One unusual gain made in spring 2008 was a seasonal flow of seed potatoes from Elgin to Ely. This traffic used the wagonload network for only part of its journey and must have incurred substantial operating costs. A more promising flow was paper from Shotton to Barking, which started in the summer and shared haulage with existing traffic between Warrington and Wembley. However, it would last only 12 months.

Overall, the wagonload network at the end of 2008 was a pale shadow of the service EWS had built up in its early years. To some extent, the wagonload concept had been a victim of competition in the railfreight market, as EWS tended to lose its higher-volume flows on some routes and be left with lower-volume traffic which was unsustainable on its own. This was particularly true in Scotland where, for example, the loss of cement flows to Aberdeen and Inverness to Freightliner Heavy Haul deprived EWS of its baseload.

As the DB Schenker logo started to make its appearance, the days of marshalling yards and trip workings were finally passing into history.

RIGHT 08844 shunts Grangemouth traffic at Daventry on 22 August 2006. Daventry was one of the most successful intermodal railheads in the early 21st century, thanks largely to its location within the 'golden triangle' of distribution warehouses in the South Midlands and its convenient access from the West Coast main line.

ABOVE 67028 approaches Arpley Junction after running round at Latchford with train 6F44, the 10.10 from Ditton to Arpley, on 12 February 2008. The loading point for this traffic was later switched from Ditton to Warrington Dallam. One of the last cross-Channel wagonload flows was chlorofluoromethane from North West England to Germany, loaded in ICA/ICB tank wagons.

LEFT Immingham sorting sidings became the gathering point for various wagonload flows of steel, paper and chemicals to and from the docks. Yard pilot 08886 shunts vans loaded with Stora Enso paper on 7 August 2002.

nine

The Channel Tunnel and Automotive

Access to the Channel Tunnel ought to have been the icing on the cake when EWS took over Railfreight Distribution in 1997. The physical assets linked to the Tunnel were substantial. As well as the purpose-built fleet of Class 92 locomotives and large numbers of automotive and intermodal wagons, EWS took control of Wembley yard with its 29 sidings and 10 miles of track, the smaller yard at Dollands Moor, used for exchanging locomotives and crews, and dedicated intermodal terminals at Willesden, Trafford Park, Wakefield and Mossend. Unfortunately, the traffic base was rather less substantial. Whereas the Tunnel had been expected to carry six million tonnes of railfreight a year by 1997, the actual figure was less than half that. The high cost of using the Tunnel and poor service quality in France had stymied growth, especially in the intermodal sector which had been expected to bring the greatest rewards.

The Channel Tunnel freight timetable in summer 1997 included an average of nine intermodal trains in each direction every day. Whereas BR had intended to run direct intermodal trains between an individual terminal in the UK and its counterpart in mainland Europe, traffic volumes were too low for that system to work and most services ran to and from Wembley yard instead, where train portions were divided and recombined as required. On the European side, roughly half of the trains ran to and from northern Italy, serving terminals at Milan Rogoredo, Melzo, Novara and Oleggio. The remainder included two daily trains to and from Muizen, one to and from Metz, one to and from Paris Valenton and a four-times-weekly train serving Lyon, Avignon and Perpignan. Some of these terminals acted as hubs for onward services to more distant locations: The ACI hub at Paris Valenton, for example, offered connections to 28 further locations in France, while Muizen provided connections to many European destinations and even to Morocco, the latter via Cadiz and Tangier.

In the UK, EWS served its own terminals at Willesden, Trafford Park, Wakefield and Mossend, as well as third-party terminals operated by Parsec at Hams Hall, Tibbett & Britten at Daventry and Freightliner at Seaforth. The Hams Hall facility took over from Birmingham Landor Street Freightliner terminal in 1997, releasing capacity at Landor Street for an increase in deep-sea business. The small amount of Channel Tunnel intermodal traffic to and from Seaforth was conveyed by a Freightliner train between Seaforth and Crewe Basford Hall yard. Willesden and Trafford Park were the busiest of the UK terminals, each handling an average of four trains a day, whereas Wakefield Euroterminal struggled to generate enough traffic for one daily train.

Automotive traffic was expected to figure prominently in the Channel Tunnel freight timetable, as the use of through trains between mainland Europe and the UK provided much quicker transit than previously possible. BR had been confident enough to introduce a fleet of 300 totally enclosed, car-carrying wagons for Tunnel traffic, permanently coupled in sets of five. Apart from eliminating the risk of vandalism, the use of totally enclosed wagons meant that cars would no longer need to be waxed before delivery, leading to savings of time and money. However, as with all freight flows via the Tunnel, the amount of business actually generated fell short of expectation.

In 1997, the Channel Tunnel carried just one flow of cars for export – a daily train of Rover vehicles from Longbridge and Cowley to Brescia in Northern Italy. This traffic had run since before the Tunnel opened and went on to provide its first ever revenue-earning freight train. Each

LEFT 08543 shunts a consignment of Land Rovers for Southampton Docks at the STVA loading point at Bordesley, loaded on French-registered IFA and IPA wagons, on 23 February 20001. At this time consideration was still being given to building a branch line to serve the Land Rover plant at Solihull, a project that was sadly never fulfilled.

BELOW 66223 approaches Leighton Buzzard with a typical mixture of swap bodies and ISO-type containers in tow, forming 4A36, the 14.15 Hams Hall to Wembley train, on 19 August 2000. Unlike Daventry, Hams Hall was located away from the electrified network and Class 92 haulage was therefore not possible.

LEFT 66238 and 66101 depart from Washwood Heath with 6O95, the 09.59 train to Dollands Moor, conveying Rover vehicles for Italy on 27 July 2000. Washwood Heath yard was the gathering point for automotive traffic from Longbridge and Bordesley to destinations at home and overseas. The yard also contained a rake of KSA 'high cube' component vans and several sets of WIA fully enclosed car carriers.

train conveyed some 200 cars and was over 2,000ft long, making it the UK's longest automotive formation. However, the Rover train did not use the fully enclosed wagons designed for Tunnel traffic but conventional Cartic-type stock, adapted for Tunnel use. As for imports, some of the Rover wagons were backloaded with Fiat cars from Italy to Avonmouth, while EWS also carried trainloads of Ford cars from Genk to Garston, and Peugeot and Citroën cars (for the logistics company GEFCO) from France to Corby and Doncaster.

The regular flow of Ford automotive components for Transfesa between Silla and Dagenham continued, conveying swap bodies on French-registered, two-axle wagons with variable gauge axles for standard and Spanish track gauges, as well as conforming to the various tunnel profile limitations of Spain, France and the UK. The original intention was for the train to serve Ford factories in Dagenham, Halewood and South Wales, but in practice it only ever ran to and from Dagenham.

The domestic automotive traffic that came with the Railfreight Distribution takeover included two main groups of services, one for Ford and the other for Rover. The Ford traffic consisted of cars from Garston to Dagenham and from Dagenham to Garston and Mossend, vans from Eastleigh to Garston and Mossend, and components between Swansea, Bridgend, Dagenham and Halewood. For Rover, cars were moved from Longbridge and Bordesley to Southampton and Purfleet for export, and body panels from Swindon to Longbridge. The body panels were carried in the recently introduced KSA 'high cube' wagons which, having a cargo hold between their bogies, enabled a higher payload per wagon than with conventional stock.

Traffic in conventional wagons was seen as a relatively minor element of Tunnel services, but in practice this business filled three daily trains in each direction between Wembley yard and northern France. Under Railfreight Distribution management a network of feeder trains had operated between Wembley and more than 20 individual terminals, carrying loads as diverse as bottled water, steel and china clay, though most flows of chemicals had ceased because of dangerous goods restrictions in the Tunnel. During 1997 the RfD network – which had been marketed as Connectrail – was gradually integrated with EWS's domestic Enterprise services, cutting out duplication on trunk routes

RIGHT Much of the freight activity at Wembley yard took place at night. 92023 *Ravel* waits with 4B45, an additional late evening departure to Melzo in northern Italy, on 22 July 1999.

ABOVE **Jaguar generated new rail traffic from both Halewood and Castle Bromwich plants. 66092 hauls empty WIAs out of the Halewood complex on 23 April 2001, just before the start of regular night-time trains from the plant.**

such as the West Coast main line as well as opening up new possibilities for both Tunnel and domestic traffic.

The overall volume of railfreight moved through the Tunnel grew under EWS management, reaching a total of 3.1 million tonnes in 1998. But that was as good as things would get. Issues of service reliability continued to undermine the confidence of customers already paying a premium to use rail rather than road. The total throughput declined to just under 2.9 million tonnes in 1999, and was only slightly higher in 2000. There were a few gains during this time, notably the start of a direct intermodal service between Bari and Trafford Park, catering mainly for imports of Italian furniture. However, the established intermodal flows to and from France, Belgium and Northern Italy were only stable at best.

In 2001, EWS and the freight division of SNCF launched a joint initiative called Channel Rail Freight to improve quality of service and attract more customers to the Tunnel. It enabled customers to buy end-to-end transits, generally at 24 hours' notice, from a single combined marketing team in London comprising both SNCF and EWS staff. Customer service was to be improved by tracking the progress of Tunnel wagons throughout their journey and informing customers of delays or other problems. Delays at that time were all too commonplace: from 1998-2000, the proportion of Italian services arriving within 60 minutes of their booked time fell from 75% to 62%.

In an effort to reduce costs and improve reliability, Channel Rail Freight restructured the timetable for intermodal services by reducing the role of Wembley yard and running most trains as a block unit between one terminal in the UK and one in mainland Europe, much as originally planned back in the late 1980s. One inevitable result of this change was a reduction in the number of route permutations. Hams Hall, for example, retained direct services only to and from Milan, whereas previously it had handled traffic to and from five or six European locations using feeders to and from Wembley. Seaforth finally lost its Tunnel intermodal service and Mossend was cut to just two intermodal departures a week. In mainland Europe, the often poorly loaded train to Avignon and Perpignan was withdrawn.

While Channel Rail Freight took useful measures to improve customer service, there was one problem over which it had only limited control: security. Increasing numbers of illegal immigrants were smuggling themselves into

ABOVE 92005 *Mozart* passes the Channel Tunnel Rail Link construction works on the outskirts of Ashford with an early morning Wembley to Dollands Moor train, conveying empty IZA, IWB and IWA vans for redistribution in mainland Europe on 31 May 2001.

containers and EWS was fined for each immigrant discovered on one of its trains. By mid-2001 these fines amounted to more than £600,000. Unfortunately, things would only get worse. In November 2001, a wave of asylum seekers invaded the yard at Calais-Fréthun and forced SNCF to drastically reduce the number of freight trains using the Tunnel. For six months EWS could only run 40% of normal services, not only causing the company to lose £10 million in potential revenue but also undermining the fragile confidence of its customers. Eventually, the security at Fréthun was improved and normal services resumed, but not before many customers made alternative arrangements for their business. Among the casualties were the Mossend to Paris train and the thrice-weekly CTL service from Trafford Park and Willesden to Paris.

Railfreight tonnages through the Tunnel recovered modestly in 2003-04, but by the end of 2004 almost all the traffic to and from northern Italy had ceased. Intercontainer also closed down its 'hub and spoke' network from Metz, which had handled some Tunnel traffic. Willesden Euroterminal was quietly mothballed, its business having declined to a trickle. EWS and Transfesa failed in their attempt to open up the Silla to Dagenham automotive train to general traffic, and renewed efforts to establish an intermodal route into Germany were unsuccessful.

By the end of 2006, overall Tunnel rail freight tonnages had fallen below those of 1995, the first full year of operation. Unilog withdrew its Muizen train in January 2007, after EWS had to change its pricing regime following the cessation of UK-French government subsidies to cover the Eurotunnel 'Minimum User Charge'. EWS also announced in 2007 that it would be launching three new routes over the following 12 months: Daventry to Brussels, Trafford Park to Duisburg, and Trafford Park to Milan. In the event, only the Trafford Park to Duisburg service got off the ground, using shared haulage and a domestic intermodal train between Trafford Park and Wembley, and wagonload services between Wembley and Duisburg. The Trafford Park to Bari train ceased in 2008, having run only intermittently during the previous year.

Automotive flows both through the Tunnel and within the UK came and went as the automotive industry evolved and altered its distribution patterns. The GEFCO traffic from France to Corby grew, reaching a maximum of eight trains a week in summer 1998. GEFCO also put some cars on rail at Sheerness, where a loading terminal in the port area had been restored to use. By the end of 1998, EWS had run trial or short-term flows of Daewoo cars from Avonmouth to Mossend, Nissan cars from Doncaster to Italy, Mazda cars from Queenborough to Selby and Glasgow Deanside, Renault cars from Southampton to Teesport, Land Rovers from Bordesley to Southampton, Ford Transit vans from Immingham to Dagenham and Avonmouth, and Case tractors from Doncaster to France.

Meanwhile, Freightliner entered the automotive market with the launch of its Autoliner operation, using collapsible 'Car-Rac' platforms that could be carried on Freightliner wagons. By the end of 1999 it had gained a share of the Ford traffic from Dagenham and Southampton to Garston and Mossend. Freightliner later moved cars from Portbury as well, but could not sustain these flows profitably and would withdraw from the automotive business in 2005.

Investment projects for EWS-operated traffic included a new automotive and intermodal terminal at Tyne Dock, which generated a weekly trainload of Nissan cars to Italy from summer 1999. Tyne Dock also received a weekly train from Avonmouth from early 2000, carrying container loads of Nissan components from Spain.

Rover traffic from Cowley resumed in 1999 after a two-year lapse but was short-lived, as Rover 75 production switched to Longbridge in 2000. However, the Cowley branch was assured a future as the plant became the production site for the new BMW Mini. In 2001, EWS introduced a daily trainload of Minis from Cowley to Purfleet for export, using fully enclosed WIA wagons. Meanwhile, Vauxhall experimented with rail after a break of several years, using Ellesmere Port as a loading point for trainloads of Astra estate cars to Purfleet from early 2000. Unfortunately, the Vauxhall traffic used open wagons and too many cars were vandalised for the business to be sustainable.

Jaguar made a major commitment to rail when it installed new loading facilities at Halewood, supported by a £1.8 million government grant. The first loaded train left the new terminal in April 2001, bound for Southampton Docks in fully enclosed WIA wagons. Jaguar's sister plant at Castle Bromwich would gain a rail connection in the following year, part-funded by a £5.3 million grant and again producing traffic for export via Southampton.

Automotive traffic played a part in two line re-openings in 2001-02. One was the long-mooted revival of the former Portishead branch to serve coal and automotive import terminals at Royal Portbury Dock. By 2002, Portbury was generating intermittent car trains to Bathgate, carrying a variety of makes including Vauxhall, Toyota and Fiat. The other addition to the network was the former colliery branch to Baddesley, which was re-laid in 2002 to serve the TNT Logistics/Volkswagen parts distribution centre at Birch Coppice. EWS introduced a daily trip working from Bescot to Birch Coppice to deliver vanloads of parts from Germany.

The collapse of Rover in 2005, following the failure of a proposed joint venture with China, brought an abrupt end to EWS's longstanding traffic from Longbridge. The Swindon to Longbridge body panel flow had already ceased in the previous year, leaving the specialised fleet of KSA 'high cube' wagons out of work. Another loss in 2005 was Ford component traffic from Swansea to Dagenham, leaving just Bridgend on the South Wales axis.

The year 2007 saw the closure of Bathgate as an automotive railhead, with Tyne Dock taking over as the receiving terminal for imported cars from Portbury. This change allowed some wagons to be backloaded more easily with Nissan cars from Tyne Dock to Portbury. Channel Tunnel automotive traffic had sunk to a significantly low level by this time, with only imports of Peugeot cars to Corby and components from Silla to Dagenham. The start-up of Honda traffic from South Marston to Ghent via the Tunnel, using fully enclosed WIA wagons, was therefore one of the year's more welcome developments.

ABOVE This typical mixture of traffic is pictured on 17 February 2003 at Trafford Park Euroterminal – one of the more successful Channel Tunnel railheads owned by EWS, although it became increasingly geared toward deep-sea and domestic traffic rather than Tunnel business.

Channel Tunnel railfreight: gross volume in million tonnes

Year	Million tonnes
1995	1.35
1996	2.78
1997	2.93
1998	3.14
1999	2.87
2000	2.95
2001	2.45
2002	1.46
2003	1.74
2004	1.89
2005	1.58
2006	1.57
2007	1.21
2008	1.24
2009	1.18
2010	1.13

ABOVE 90018 waits in the loop at Acton Bridge with 6L48, the 14.50 Garston to Dagenham empties, on 2 June 2006. For several years, the Dagenham to Garston automotive flow was the only freight train that regularly produced EWS Class 90 haulage.

RIGHT 66034 stands at the west end of Dollands Moor yard with 6M26, the 10.20 departure to Corby, on 31 May 2001. This train originated at Achères yard in Paris and conveyed cars from several Peugeot-Citroën factories for the British market. 92009 and 92035 are awaiting their next Wembley-bound duty.

ABOVE 08685 crawls out of Doncaster Railport on 21 July 2006 with Citroën cars and vans for Belmont yard, a trip that required a run-round movement at St Catherine's Junction to avoid crossing the East Coast main line on the level.

LEFT 67030 ambles along the reopened Birch Coppice branch with 6G42, the 11.23 Birch Coppice to Bescot feeder service, on 28 July 2006. This train conveyed empty vans to Germany that had carried spare Volkswagen parts.

ABOVE 60034 waits to depart from Prologis Park with empty vans forming 6A51, the 11.50 train to Wembley, on 29 May 2007. The Prologis Park rail hub on the site of Coventry colliery was slow to attract railfreight traffic, but for a time it handled trainloads of bottled water from France.

LEFT 66058 snakes through the yard at Ripple Lane, ready to cross over onto the Dagenham freight lines with 7L23, the 04.17 Dollands Moor to Dagenham Transfesa car parts train, on 30 August 2006. With its variable gauge IFA and IFB wagons facilitating through running to and from Spain, this train was restricted to 45mph in the UK and therefore ran Class 7.

RIGHT 92012 and 92010 stand at Fréthun, awaiting their Tunnel path with a 1,461-tonne trainload of water bound ultimately for Neasden on 31 May 2001. Bottled water from France provided some of the longest trains through the Channel Tunnel.

012

ten

Mail and Parcels

Royal Mail traffic accounted for roughly two thirds of the £75 million a year turnover of Rail Express Systems (RES) when it passed into Wisconsin Central ownership in December 1995. The business employed 800 staff, had 20 electric and over 100 diesel locomotives on its books, and operated five train-crew depots as well as four traction and rolling stock maintenance depots.

LEFT 67008 passes Dawlish Warren with 1E41, the 17.23 Plymouth to Low Fell train, on 18 July 2000. The West Country was well served by mail trains, mainly because of the long-distance traffic on offer.

RIGHT Locomotive haulage of the Royal Mail Class 325 units came in useful for diversions caused by engineering work or by an emergency. On 25 August 2000 67001 passes South Milford with units 325015 and 325002 in tow, forming 1M78, the 14.39 Low Fell to Willesden train, diverted away from the East Coast main line because of a derailment.

The future for mail by rail looked good, as in December 1993 Royal Mail had signed a 10-year contract with BR for a revised network of services, named Railnet, which would come into effect in September 1996. Under the terms of that contract, Royal Mail and RES invested £180 million in new rolling stock and terminals.

Most of the cash went on the construction of 16 Class 325 electric multiple units, which would remain in Royal Mail ownership but would be operated by RES. The dual-voltage capability of the '325s' meant that they could work on the dc third-rail route from London to Dover, as well as on the ac overhead West and East Coast main lines. They could also be hauled by diesel locomotives, giving them useful flexibility when diverted away from their scheduled route due to engineering work or a temporary line blockage.

Railnet's investment in terminals involved the building of eight rail hubs, which replaced the shared use of passenger stations at strategic locations. The central hub was the seven-platform Princess Royal Distribution Centre (PRDC) at Willesden, which opened on 30 September 1996. Serving a large swathe of South East England as well as Heathrow Airport, the PRDC had the capacity to process 34 trains and 400 road vehicles per day. Further Royal Mail hubs were located at Low Fell, Tonbridge, Doncaster, Motherwell, Warrington, Stafford and Bristol. Mail trains also continued to use passenger stations on some parts of the network, such as South Wales and the far South West.

For Travelling Post Office (TPO) trains and mail trains on non-electrified routes, hauled stock remained the norm. Ex-BR GUV and BG vehicles, some of which dated back to the late 1950s, were refurbished to allow the roll-on/roll-off use of York containers. The cost and inconvenience of run-round movements was avoided by the introduction of Propelling Control Vehicles, converted from Class 307 driving trailers and positioned at the opposite end of the train to the locomotive. As for the traction, Classes 86 and 90 continued to operate on electrified routes, but EWS needed to find a replacement for its ageing Class 47 diesels. An order for 30 Class '67's fulfilled that need; they entered service between late 1999 and April 2000, releasing the RES '47s' for redeployment or withdrawal.

LEFT The TPO train between London and Dover was rostered for top-and-tail Class 73 traction. 73131 heads 1090, the 16.30 Willesden to Dover train, through Kensington Olympia on 23 August 2000, with sister locomotive 73128 bringing up the rear.

ABOVE 90016 speeds north at South Kenton, still in Rail Express Systems livery, with 1S96, the 16.00 Willesden to Shieldmuir train, on 15 July 2002.

RIGHT The premium logistics trains used Class 67 haulage both on the West Coast main line and on the extensions to Aberdeen and Inverness. 67007 pauses for a crew change at Motherwell while working 1S03, the 00.39 Walsall to Aberdeen train, on 27 August 2003.

RIGHT EWS refurbished a small fleet of ex-BR parcels vans for its premium logistics services, linking the West Midlands with central and northern Scotland. Unloading is taking place at Inverness Millburn yard on 21 August 2001, just one week after the service was extended to the highland capital. GAVIN MORRISON

The signing of a 10-year contract and Royal Mail's ownership of the Class 325 fleet did not prevent the corporation questioning its use of rail. After carrying out a thorough review, Consignia – the short-lived trading name of Royal Mail at that time – announced in 2002 that it was pulling out of sorting mail on the move, putting an end to the remaining TPO services that ran from Willesden to Dover, Low Fell, Plymouth, Carlisle, Swansea and Norwich, and on cross-country routes from Penzance to Bristol, Bristol to Low Fell and Cardiff to Shieldmuir. Worse news came in June 2003, when Royal Mail announced it was withdrawing completely from rail. Not only did this mean cutting short the contract with EWS, but also mothballing the Class 325 electric units after just seven years in service. The decision was largely determined by cost, even though EWS had reduced its price by 20%.

During 2003, the network of TPO and other mail trains was gradually wound down. The last TPO train reached its destination on 20 January 2004, with just a few residual services for pre-sorted mail continuing into February. The PRDC at Willesden was retained for road traffic, as were the Royal Mail terminals at Warrington and Shieldmuir, but other depots were abandoned, including Bristol Parkway which had opened just two years previously. The Class 325 units went into storage, along with the large fleet of TPO and other hauled stock that had been used mainly on non-electrified routes.

While the prospects for future Royal Mail traffic looked bleak, EWS was developing a separate network of high-speed services for other parcel carriers. Following trials in 2000 between Wolverhampton and Law Junction with a Class 90 locomotive and seven 110mph vans, the company built a dedicated parcels terminal at Walsall Tasker Street and, by the end of 2001, was operating a nightly train from Walsall to Aberdeen with a connecting service from Law Junction to Inverness. A three-year contract with logistics company DHL provided a reliable baseload for these trains. It was a flagship operation for EWS and featured regularly on the front page of the company's *Customer First* publication.

In 2003, EWS received a £650,000 grant from the Scottish Executive towards the £1 million cost of a new parcels terminal at Mossend, which would replace Law Junction, and the company later won an award for innovation from *International Freighting Weekly* on account of its new flexible lightweight design of parcel cage. Hopes of further growth in the premium parcels sector were raised when the company purchased 14 former Mk III sleeping cars for possible conversion to parcels vans. With their maximum speed of 125mph, they would enable EWS to offer a London to Edinburgh service in less than four hours. Unfortunately, the proposal failed to generate sufficient commercial interest; in February 2007, DHL switched its business to road and EWS closed down its entire premium parcels operation as a result.

The running of a few pre-Christmas 'extras' between Willesden and Shieldmuir in 2007, using Class 90 traction and a mixture of GUV and BG stock, appeared to be EWS's final involvement in Royal Mail trains. However, in December 2004, GB Railfreight had revived a limited mail service on the West Coast main line, using some of the previously mothballed Royal Mail Class 325 units. The contract for these trains would switch to EWS's successor – DB Schenker – in 2010.

eleven

Infrastructure Traffic

In British Rail days, infrastructure – or 'departmental' – traffic, such as the carrying of railway ballast, spoil, sleepers and rails, was not part of the revenue-earning railfreight business at all. The running of infrastructure trains was a requirement placed on operations by regional civil engineers, and resources were made freely available by depot and train-crew managers.

LEFT 37703 arrives at Oxford Hinksey yard with two ZFV 'Dogfish' wagons on 2 July 1999. Many vacuum-braked wagons were still in use on infrastructure flows at the end of the 20th century.

RIGHT Mainline-liveried loco 37274 arrives at the docks with 7B05, the 09.07 empties from Eastleigh yard, on 20 July 1998. The virtual quarry at Southampton Docks received granite ballast by sea from Glensanda, for onward distribution by rail.

This all changed with privatisation. The splitting of infrastructure from operations signalled the end of the long-established departmental culture; new business relationships had to be established between the owner of the railway and the providers of train services required to maintain and renew it. It was never seriously envisaged that Railtrack would become a train operator itself.

When Trainload Freight was prepared for sale to the private sector in 1994, the government had placed a contractual requirement on the three bulk freight companies – Loadhaul, Mainline Freight and Transrail – to carry infrastructure traffic for Railtrack within their defined geographical area. The three companies were also required to collaborate with each other in maintaining a national train network for sub-trainload infrastructure traffic. For network trains serving permanent locations such as quarries, spoil tips and sleeper depots, the freight operators held contracts with Railtrack; for possession trains servicing engineering work sites, however, the operators held tripartite contracts involving 13 engineering companies, as well as Railtrack.

Once Loadhaul, Mainline Freight and Transrail came together as EWS, the organisation of the network trains for Railtrack became more straightforward. However, the fact that each of the 13 engineering companies chose its own source of infrastructure materials – such as ballast – meant that EWS found itself running numerous short trains to and from a large number of locations, while the costs per tonne of materials moved were high. In 1997, Railtrack initiated a wide-reaching review of its infrastructure train operations, its main objective being to rationalise the network of materials supply trains by concentrating traffic on core routes. This was similar to the policy that Trainload Freight had successfully adopted for commercial freight in the early 1990s.

The 1997 review resulted in the formation of 16 local distribution centres (LDCs), each acting as a focus for assembling and disassembling possession trains within its defined area. In operational terms the LDCs were similar to marshalling yards; some had long-established associations with infrastructure traffic, such as Guide Bridge and Carnforth, while others were new locations on the infrastructure map, like Oxford Hinksey.

The review also led to the creation of 'virtual quarries', i.e. stockpiles of ballast and other infrastructure materials at locations close to their eventual point of use. In the past, the only stockpiles of ballast had been at the quarries themselves and loaded wagons would carry the ballast all the way to the engineering possession. It was an inefficient system as far as wagon utilisation was concerned, especially when the quarry was a long way from the possession. Where possible, therefore, the virtual quarries were situated within LDCs so that the number of train movements was kept

LEFT 60064 nears its destination with 6K22 from Penmaenmawr to Basford Hall on 30 August 2000. EWS continued to transport ballast on this route for some time after Freightliner took over the operation of Basford Hall yard.

LEFT 66065 passes the disused wagon repair shops at Toton on 21 July 2008 with 6K50, the 15.12 Toton to Crewe infrastructure train. The wagons comprise one empty YLA rail carrier, five HQA 'Autoballasters' and five JJA 'Autoballasters'.

RIGHT 66211 passes Hardrigg with a rake of MRA side-tipping ballast wagons on 6 June 2007 to form 6K05, the 13.22 Carlisle to Crewe infrastructure train. Both EWS and Freightliner Heavy Haul operated infrastructure trains on this route.

to a minimum. However, in a few locations the virtual quarry and its associated LDC were several miles apart, such as Grain and Hoo Junction or Purfleet and Temple Mills.

EWS and Railtrack took the opportunity to rationalise the number of quarries supplying ballast. Some familiar locations disappeared from the map, including Shap, Hartshill and Meldon, while each of the six quarries which remained in use was contracted to supply a quantity of ballast to make the provision of a regular train service viable.

EWS also moved spoil, rail, sleepers and contractors' equipment. The principal spoil tips were located at Tyne Yard, Ince Moss, Doncaster, Chaddesden, Connington, Theale, Purfleet, Grain and Eastleigh. Long-welded rail was forwarded directly from British Steel Track Products at Workington and the British Steel welding plant at Castleton. Concrete sleepers were supplied by Tarmac at Tallington and Coltness, and by RMC at Washwood Heath, while wooden sleepers were produced by Phoenix at Ditton.

EWS inherited a diverse fleet of mainly elderly wagons for infrastructure traffic. Many were cast-offs from the BR revenue-earning wagon fleet. Out of a total of 6,000 vehicles, roughly one third were fitted with vacuum brakes, which made them incompatible with modern locomotives. EWS therefore launched a £6 million programme to refurbish and renew its infrastructure wagon fleet. By 1998, 300 ZCA Sea Urchins had been converted from redundant SPA steel wagons, 400 MHA open-box wagons had been built on the underframes of HAA/HEA coal hoppers, and 200 MTA low-sided box wagons for spoil had been converted using the underframes of redundant Shell Oil tankers. American-style swing-motion bogies were fitted to 125 YEA bogie rail wagons to increase their speed from 45 to 60mph. Renewing the fleet was a large operation, and the last vacuum-braked wagons would not be retired until summer 2001.

Not all the wagons used on infrastructure flows were owned by EWS. The Redland self-discharge train was used for some ballast drops in possessions. Successful trials were carried out with 10 power-door discharge 'Autoballaster' wagons converted from Tiphook KPA hoppers, and Railtrack started to build up its stock of hired open box wagons to carry stone from quarries – starting with an order for 120 bogie JNAs and 250 two-axle PNAs.

While most infrastructure flows remained a hostage to rail transport, that did not assure EWS a monopoly of the Railtrack (and later Network Rail) business. In July 1999, Freightliner hit the headlines when it signed an eight-year contract to provide traction for Railtrack's track construction and renewal programme. That contract kick-started Freightliner's Heavy Haul

RIGHT 66075 snakes out of the Corus Rail welding depot at Castleton with 6E70, the 12.01 departure to Doncaster, on 2 September 2002. The long-welded rail, carried on nine YEA 'Perch' wagons, is destined for infrastructure renewal sites at Stukeley and Huddersfield.

division and marked the company's first significant incursion into EWS territory. As part of the deal, Freightliner became the operator of Crewe LDC and would haul some of Railtrack's most specialised kit, including the Track Renewal Train and the High Output Ballast Cleaner.

Over the ensuing years, Network Rail not only divided its haulage contracts between EWS and Freightliner but also awarded some work to GB Railfreight – who achieved a breakthrough by becoming the operator of the new Whitemoor LDC in 2004. Nevertheless, infrastructure movements remained an important part of the EWS portfolio. At the end of 2008, the company still hauled the majority of timetabled ballast trains across the network and was the sole infrastructure operator in several areas, including Scotland and South Wales. EWS also won some non-Network Rail infrastructure business, including a contract to supply ballast for the rebuilding of the Metrolink line between Manchester and Bury in 2007.

Virtual Quarries and Local Distribution Centres, 1998

Quarry	Virtual quarry	Local distribution centre
Cloburn (by road)	Carstairs	Mossend Millerhill
Mountsorrel	Tyne Yard Doncaster Toton Peterborough	Tyne Yard Doncaster Toton Peterborough
Penmaenmawr	Carnforth Guide Bridge	Carnforth Guide Bridge
Stud Farm	Bescot Rugby Hinksey	Bescot Rugby Hinksey
Machen	-	Newport
Glensanda (by sea)	Southampton Westbury (via Southampton) Purfleet Grain	Eastleigh Westbury Temple Mills Hoo Junction

twelve

Not Just Freight

Significantly, the name English Welsh & Scottish Railway did not include the word 'freight'. The company was keen to seek business opportunities in all areas of railway operation and services. In order to grasp and develop these opportunities, EWS launched its Rail Services division. Its remit included not only Rail Express Systems but also such diverse operations as engineering sales, charter trains, rolling stock leasing company (ROSCO) train haulage, Railtest and the Royal Train.

LEFT One of the most photographed passenger trains of 2004 was the Arriva service on the Settle to Carlisle line, which produced a pair of EWS Class 37s and refurbished Mk II rolling stock. 37408 and 37411 provide the power for the southbound train as it crosses Arten Gill viaduct on 8 September.

RIGHT 47786 stands at Aberdeen on 16 July 1999 with the 21.40 departure to London Euston. ScotRail did not operate any locomotives of its own and used EWS traction on its sleeper services.
HUGH BALLANTYNE

In 1997, engineering sales provided the second biggest earner for Rail Services, covering the maintenance of locomotives and rolling stock for other operators – including 50 Class 47s for Freightliner and 25 of the same for CrossCountry trains. These locomotives were based at Crewe alongside the EWS fleet of '47s' used on RES trains, which were subject to stringent reliability standards to fulfil the Royal Mail contract.

Charter train haulage had passed from InterCity to RES in 1994. The shift made good sense because RES was a national operator, whereas the InterCity network was broken up into regional franchises. If the charter business had passed to any of the InterCity franchise holders, that company would have had to buy in resources to provide a nationwide service. Charter trains came in many guises, ranging from exclusive 'hotels on wheels' such as the *Royal Scotsman* and luxury trains like the *Venice Simplon Orient Express* to more modest services for sporting events or exhibitions.

In the early 1990s the number of charter trains had reached around 500 a year, but this number fell after privatisation because the business now had to cover previously hidden costs and some types of operation were no longer viable. Nevertheless, EWS saw the charter market as having reasonable long-term prospects, especially as it used some resources at weekends which would otherwise have been standing idle.

The contract to haul empty rolling stock for the ROSCOs had been awarded to RES in April 1995. When EWS took over the operation it amounted to roughly 45 movements a week. Some trains operated on a regular timetabled basis, such as those carrying coaching stock between Willesden and Springburn for maintenance, while others were one-off services organised as and when required.

RES had also gained the Railtest contract trains in April 1995, running up to 40 trains a week alongside various other Railtest activities including rail grinding, track gauging and vehicle testing. This work foreshadowed the operation of seasonal railhead treatment trains, using high-pressure water and Sandite solution to clear autumn leaves on many parts of the network.

The Royal Train was arguably the jewel in the crown of the Rail Services portfolio. RES had taken over its operation in April 1994 and its proven quality of service had enabled access to the national rail network. The fact that two Class 47 locomotives were dedicated to its use showed how important the contract was. However, the Royal Train was regarded by many as an unnecessarily expensive luxury and a thorough review of its cost-effectiveness was carried out in 2003. Thankfully, Britain's most prestigious train survived that review and EWS rebranded two Class 67 locomotives in royal claret livery to allow the phasing out of the Class 47s.

The haulage of scheduled passenger trains was fertile ground for EWS. In the early days, Class 37 and 47 locomotives fitted with electric train heating were used on various routes

LEFT 37298 and 37796 are pictured in top-and-tail mode on an engineering train at Eurre on 31 August 1999, on the Rhône Valley extension of the Mediterranean *ligne à grande vitesse*. EWS hired out many surplus locomotives for railway infrastructure projects in mainland Europe.

LEFT The first West Yorkshire Class 333 unit, 333001, is pictured at Normanton on its way from Wakefield Europort to Neville Hill depot on 11 March 2000, headed by EWS 56114 with 56018 bringing up the rear. GAVIN MORRISON

RIGHT 37428 and 37427 pass through Paddock cutting, Huddersfield, with a Scottish Railway Preservation Society special running as 1Z37, the 04.16 from Linlithgow to Shrewsbury, on 31 May 2003. 37428 had received *Royal Scotsman* claret livery in 1998, but worked a wide range of service trains and excursions until taken out of service in December 2003. GAVIN MORRISON

including sleeper services north of Edinburgh, First North Western trains to and from the North Wales coast, Arriva trains on the Settle & Carlisle line and Arriva trains in South Wales. The use of Class 37s on the Rhymney branch continued until 2006. EWS also provided '47s' as 'thunderbird' locomotives to rescue failed passenger trains on various parts of the network, including the West and East Coast main lines.

As for electrics, ScotRail contracted EWS to provide Class 90 haulage on sleeper services on the West Coast main line. A specific pool of locomotives received First ScotRail branding for this work. In 2004, EWS began supplying Class 90s as cover on the London to Norwich route and, in the same year, a Class 90-hauled formation even found short-term use on the North Berwick branch.

The premature ending of the Royal Mail contract left EWS with an embarrassingly large fleet of Class 67 locomotives seeking gainful employment. A few members of the fleet were already hired to ScotRail for its sleeper services to Aberdeen and Inverness; the Fort William sleeper train went over to '67' haulage in 2006, once the necessary radio electronic token block equipment had been fitted to enable them to operate on that line. The 125mph capability of the '67s' made them well suited to 'thunderbird' duties on the East Coast main line.

In April 2008, the new open-access passenger operator Wrexham Shropshire & Marylebone Railway Company (WSMR) introduced its service between London and Wrexham, using EWS Class 67 locomotives. Initially, each train operated with a pair of '67s' in top-and-tail mode, pending the delivery of WSMR driving van trailers. First Great Western also made significant use of '67s' and EWS-owned Mk II coaches in 2007-08. These were used on a Saturdays-only summer working from Bristol to Weymouth, special trains from London Paddington to the Cheltenham races, and extra workings to Castle Cary for the Glastonbury festival.

Even redundant locomotives could earn money. In 1999, EWS sent 40 Class 37s to Eurre in France to haul infrastructure trains on a new stretch of high-speed railway. In 2001, a pool of 15 Class 37s went to Spain for a similar purpose, joined later by a small pool of '58s'. Subsequently, two '37s' were exported to Italy for infrastructure duties and several '58s' found further employment in the Netherlands on container trains, while in 2004, EWS won a contract with Keolis to supply 40 Class 56 and 58 locomotives for infrastructure trains on the new high-speed route between Paris and Strasbourg.

RIGHT EWS Class 37s had regular duties in South Wales, not only on the Rhymney branch but also extending as far west as Fishguard. On 8 August 2003, 37417 enters Clarbeston Road station with the 13.35 Fishguard to Rhymney service. GAVIN MORRISON

From September 2005, the leasing of its locomotives for infrastructure projects in mainland Europe came under the control of EWS subsidiary Axiom Rail, which also provided a range of rolling stock services including routine maintenance, inspection, stabling, refuelling and cleaning of passenger vehicles.

Another development that did not fall directly into the freight category was the formation of Railway Approvals Limited, based in Derby, to carry out the approval of rail vehicles for use in the UK and throughout Europe. In November 2005, EWS purchased the entire shareholding of Marcroft Engineering Limited – the well-established UK supplier of freight-wagon maintenance services, with its main workshops in Stoke-on-Trent and a number of other smaller sites across Britain.

But in many ways the most exciting development for EWS – and arguably one which would rescue the company during the dark days of recession in the early 21st century – was its move into mainland Europe with the formation of Euro Cargo Rail (ECR) in 2006. ECR began by competing for trainload freight traffic in France and achieved remarkable success. In barely two years it would gain more than 5% of the total French railfreight market, operating in sectors as diverse as agriculture, fuel, building materials and steel.

RIGHT The Wrexham Shropshire & Marylebone service provided useful passenger work for the EWS Class 67s, especially in the early days when driving trailers were not available and all trains had to have a locomotive at each end. 67013 is pictured just after leaving Wrexham with the 18.10 to London Marylebone on 14 May 2008; 67028 is bringing up the rear.

ABOVE 47793 *Christopher Wren passes* Basford Hall yard, Crewe, with the 06.45 from Holyhead to Birmingham New Street on 14 August 2003. Locomotive haulage had returned to the North Wales coast in 2002 as a result of a shortage of diesel units.

RIGHT The Royal Train survived a stringent expenditure review and continued to find its way to many corners of Network Rail – and beyond. The two locomotives painted in Royal claret livery, 67005 and 67006, provide the power for the return visit by HRH Prince Charles to the Severn Valley Railway from Bridgnorth to London Euston on 10 June 2008. The train is pictured descending towards Eardington. HUGH BALLANTYNE